Retirement Income Planning

Keith Popplewell ACCI, ACIB, APMI, MSFA

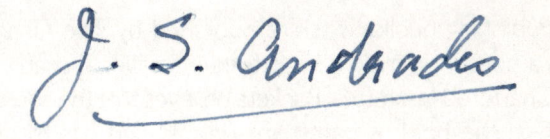

institute of financial services

Apart from any fair dealing for the purpose of research or private study, or criticism or review, as permitted under the Copyright, Designs and Patents Act 1988, this publication may be reproduced, stored or transmitted, in any form or by any means, only with the prior permission in writing of the publisher, or in the case of reprographic reproduction in accordance with the terms and licences issued by the Copyright Licensing Agency. Enquiries concerning reproduction outside those terms should be addressed to the publisher's agents at the following address:

CIB Publishing
c/o The Chartered Institute of Bankers
Emmanuel House
4-9 Burgate Lane
Canterbury
Kent
CT1 2XJ
United Kingdom

Telephone: 01227 762600

CIB Publishing publications are published by The Chartered Institute of Bankers, a non-profit making registered educational charity.

The Chartered Institute of Bankers believes that the sources of information upon which the book is based are reliable and has made every effort to ensure the complete accuracy of the text. However, neither CIB, the author nor any contributor can accept any legal responsibility whatsoever for consequences that may arise from errors or omissions or any opinion or advice given.

Typeset by Kevin O'Connor
Printed by Haynes Publishing, Somerset
© Chartered Institute of Bankers 2000
ISBN 0-85297-547-3

Contents

	Introduction	v
1	Pension Schemes – A Structure	1
2	Personal Pension Arrangements	15
3	Occupational Pension Schemes	41
4	Basis of Conventional Annuities	60
5	Definition of Spouse and Dependant	83
6	With Profit and Unit-Linked Annuities	95
7	Staggered Pensions Vesting	105
8	Personal Pensions Drawdown	123
9	Flexible Annuities within Occupational Pension Schemes	146
10	Comparative Factors in Retirement Options	156
	Appendix 1: Inland Revenue Rules Relating to Maximum Benefits for Service of less than 40 years with an Employer	165
	Appendix 2: Inland Revenue Rules Relating to Maximum Benefits for Early Retirement when less than 40 years Service	172
	Appendix 3: Retained Benefits from Previous Employments	175
	Index	177

Introduction

The range of options available to an individual seeking to use an accumulated pension fund at retirement, in the most appropriate way for his or her needs is now vast. Not so long ago an individual would have been forced to buy a conventional annuity, with a limited range of choices as to how that annuity was to be paid, for example, the frequency of payments.

Nowadays he or she may be able to choose from a (sometimes bewildering) variety of policies and strategies with names such as staggered vesting, income drawdown, with profits annuity, and many more such innovative ideas. With innovation has come, unfortunately, increasing complexity.

In the first section of the book (up to Chapter 3) we look at the rules governing the benefits which may be taken from the different types of pension schemes. In particular we consider the various Inland Revenue limits on the ages at which benefits may be taken and the maximum permitted level of those benefits.

If you are reading this book with a specific pension fund in mind (rather than reading for general education purposes), please refer first to Chapter 1 to identify which type of pension scheme is involved and, therefore, which of the following two chapters must be studied. It is not necessary to read the chapters which do not relate to your particular scheme.

Moreover it should not be necessary for you to read and understand all of the chapter relevant to your scheme. As an example, some of the more complex parts of the occupational pension scheme chapter relate to the way in which retained benefits (in ordinary terms, 'previous pension schemes') may limit the level of benefits which can be taken from the current scheme. If you have no retained benefits then, quite simply, this section is superfluous to your reading.

Thus, in this first section of the book, selectivity of reading will help you cut through the need to read what, for you, would be superfluous detail.

In the second section of the book, covering Chapters 4 and 5, we look at fundamental issues relating to conventional annuities, and issues which also

v

have importance to all of the retirement income options – in particular the definition of spouse and dependant.

In the final section of the book, from Chapter 6 onwards, we describe and discuss the features of what might be described as 'flexible annuities': recent (within the last decade or so, generally) developments offering a greater degree of flexibility than conventional annuities, though almost invariably bringing greater risk with that flexibility.

Overall, you might consider that the weighting of this book demonstrates some preference towards the last section – flexible annuities – but I would like to stress this is not the case. Simply, they are more complex and far less understood than their conventional alternatives, and so merit greater explanation and discussion. Moreover, it is my belief that these alternatives may be highly attractive to many retirees and, when used, monitored, and serviced correctly can frequently offer tremendous opportunities with quantifiable level of risk.

I hope you will find this book interesting and profitable, and would ask you to tolerate certain sections which necessarily are more detailed and complex than some readers might have preferred.

1 Pension Schemes – A Structure

INTRODUCTION

There is a great variety of names and titles of pension schemes and contracts in this country and those who do not consider themselves to be pensions specialists could be forgiven for fearing that to achieve even a basic understanding of the majority of these schemes, a great deal of study and effort would be required. But this is not so.

In fact, all but an exceptionally small number of schemes can be considered as falling into one of only five categories – each category having its particular individual set of characteristics and rules. Thus when one has a working knowledge of these five categories, and knows which types of pension scheme fall into which category, it is relatively straightforward to summarize most of the essential features of almost every type of pension scheme.

It is *not* the intention of this chapter (nor, indeed, of the book as a whole) to attempt to provide comprehensive detail of any type of pension scheme, let alone *every* one – that would take many books to come anywhere near achieving. It *is* the intention, though, to give as in-depth a working awareness (rather than knowledge) of the most common types of pension scheme, allowing an understanding of the technical and subjective factors that affect a retiree's choice from the range of retirement income options.

However, certain detailed aspects of pension schemes are crucial to an understanding of various retirement income options and, where this applies, these are considered in much more depth in Chapters 2 (personal pensions) and 3 (occupational pensions).

THE THREE PILLARS OF PENSION PLANNING IN THE UK

Although not universally known by this descriptive title it is nonetheless convenient to and comprehensively accurate to consider each pension contract as being either:
- a pension provided by the state; or
- an occupational pension scheme; or
- a personal pension scheme.

State pensions
State pensions are easy to identify and categorize, comprising currently only two types of pension: the basic state pension and the state second tier pension – the latter commonly known as SERPS (the State Earnings Related Pension Scheme).

Occupational pensions
Occupational pension schemes generally describe schemes established by and, importantly, *run by* employers with one or more of their employees forming the membership of the scheme.

Personal pensions
Personal pensions are pension contracts between an individual and a pension provider. There are grey areas between these two categories which require clarification as to their proper categorization – most notably AVCs and FSAVCs (which are occupational schemes, in spite of appearing to be personal – individual – contracts) and group personal pensions (which are established by an employer but which nonetheless are really just groups of personal pensions).

All pension schemes in this country fall into one of these categories.

PENSION BENEFIT STRUCTURES

Having identified (which we soon shall, in this account) within which *pillar* a

particular scheme falls we then need to identify how the scheme calculates and pays pension benefits. There are, by coincidence, three main methods of calculating benefits (in fact, hardly any schemes calculate benefits by a method other than one of these three):
- flat rate;
- defined benefit (commonly known as *final salary*);
- defined contribution (commonly known as *money purchase*).

Flat rate

Within these types of pension scheme the fundamental principle is that all members receive the same level of pension benefit, regardless of the level of their pre-retirement income. This is not strictly true with certain flat rate schemes, however, because there may be qualification rules under which, for example, the full level of the flat rate pension might be granted only to those with a certain number of years' membership of the scheme with a lower rate payable to those with lesser number of years' membership – this being true of the (flat rate) basic state pension, as noted later in this chapter.

Defined benefit

As the name implies these schemes define, at outset, the level of pension payable to scheme members, almost invariably as a percentage or fraction of their earned income towards or at the end of their working life (typical of many large occupational pension schemes), or as a fraction of some averaging of their earnings throughout their working lifetime (for example, benefits under the State Earnings Related Pension Scheme – SERPS).

Although the level of the *employees'* contributions to these schemes will be stated (for example, 5% of salary) it is down to the employer to make sufficient additional contributions to ensure the benefit promise can be met from the scheme funds – thus his contribution level will fluctuate from time to time depending primarily on the investment performance of the pension fund.

Defined contribution

Here the contributions, both employee and employer (or by an individual within a personal pension type policy) are stated ('defined') but the eventual level of pension benefit is unknown: this will depend not only on the continuing level of contribution over the years, but also on the investment performance of the accumulating fund and the annuity rate applicable when the fund is *vested* (i.e. when benefits start to be taken).

Perhaps the most important difference between defined benefit and defined contribution schemes is that, with the former, investment and annuity rate risk is the problem of the *scheme* (as noted above, including many large employers) whereas with the latter method those risks rest with the *scheme member*.

THE PENSIONS GRID

So, every (or almost every) pension scheme in this country can be identified as being within one of the three pillars and, further, offering benefits in one of the three main ways. We can therefore suggest you 'pigeon-hole' your thinking to confirm that every type of pension scheme will fall within one of the squares in the following grid:

	Benefit Paying Method		
	Flat Rate	**Defined Benefit**	**Defined Contribution**
Pensions 'pillar'			
State-provided			
Occupational			
Personal			

FILLING IN THE PENSIONS GRID

Before we start to describe what all of this terminology means, and identify where each scheme fits, it might be encouraging to note that there are some boxes within this grid into which *no* type of pension scheme fits. We can therefore cross these off, as follows:

Benefit Paying Method

Pensions 'pillar'	Flat Rate	Defined Benefit	Defined Contribution
State-provided			✗
Occupational			
Personal	✗	✗	

Now, you can see that we only have six boxes to 'worry about', although it is very tempting to also cross out the box relating to *flat rate and occupational* as there are very few schemes that fall into this category. I have resisted the temptation to delete this box as one such scheme (for building workers) covers a very large number of members, although only for piffling levels of benefit.

STATE PENSIONS

State pensions, generally
There are only two main types of pension scheme provided by the state: the basic state retirement pension (often known as the 'old age pension') and the State Earnings Related Pension Scheme (SERPS), which is made available only to employees (thereby excluding the self-employed and the unemployed).

Entitlement to benefits from both schemes depends on the individual's National Insurance contribution record and is not in any way *means tested*. In other words, it really does not matter how much or little income or capital the individual enjoys, he or she either will or will not be entitled to benefit from one or both of the state pension benefits solely according to the National Insurance record.

State flat rate
The basic state pension is payable at a flat rate of benefit, with qualifying rules for entitlement to the full rate (broadly, a National Insurance contribution record for at least 90% of the claimant's working lifetime).

This benefit is important to retirement income planning generally as, at the full rate of around £3,500 per annum, the equivalent annuity from an insurance company – noting that the benefit escalates every year in line with increases in the Retail Prices Index, and also that a surviving spouse's pension is payable – would cost well over £50,000.

However, apart from noting its importance there are little or no planning implications apart from the ability to defer taking this benefit beyond state pension age in return for an eventual slightly increased level of benefit. We therefore have included no further mention of this scheme in this book, where we concentrate on the aspects of pensions open to the retiree's discretion.

State defined benefit
The State Earnings Related Pension Scheme is a defined benefit scheme, with pensions payable at a level depending on the claimant's average earnings during his or her working lifetime (depending on the dates of his or her membership of SERPS this may take into account all working years, or only some of them).

Pension Schemes – A Structure

The method of calculating SERPS benefits is complex, and certainly beyond the scope of this book. Insofar as SERPS is a state benefit not capable of being changed by an individual retiring member or his or her advisers there may seem little point including further discussion in this book. However, it is possible for an individual (either alone, or as part of a larger group pension scheme) to contract out ('opt out') of membership of SERPS in favour of directing equivalent contributions (collected, ordinarily, as part of National Insurance contributions) to a private pension arrangement (whether occupational or personal).

However, those contracting out of SERPS are bound, for this part of their pension fund, by certain additional rules and restrictions not applying to the main part of their pension fund. For this reason we have included some significant discussion around contracting out and the treatment of that part of pension funds – particularly at retirement – in the relevant parts of Chapters 2 (personal pension) and 3 (occupational pension).

State defined contribution

As mentioned earlier, no state pension scheme benefits use the defined contribution method of funding.

The pensions grid revisited

We can now complete the grid for all state pension benefits, as follows:

Benefit Paying Method

Pensions 'pillar'	Flat Rate	Defined Benefit	Defined Contribution
State-provided	Basic state pension	SERPS	✗
Occupational			
Personal	✗	✗	

7

OCCUPATIONAL PENSIONS

Flat rate
There are very few schemes operated by employers that pay benefits on a flat rate basis, the most notable exception being an industry-wide (meaning that the scheme covers the employees of a large number of companies in the same type of industry) occupational pension offering relatively very modest flat-rate contributions to building workers, This scheme, by the way, was established in recognition of the fact that many of these members change employers much more frequently than employees in other industries and professions and so would otherwise have little opportunity or encouragement to establish a scheme that would see them through their working lifetime.

Nonetheless, in spite of the high level of membership of this scheme the level of retirement benefits is negligible. To the best of the author's knowledge this is the only sizeable occupational scheme offering flat rate benefits, hence my earlier comment about being tempted to simplify the situation and state that no scheme fell within the occupational/flat rate box.

Defined benefit
Until just a few years ago the vast majority of pension schemes offered by medium and large companies granted benefits related to each individual member's final remuneration (although the definition of 'final' may be interpreted in different ways, and so can 'remuneration', as we discuss in Chapter 3). Increasingly over recent years, however, more and more of these schemes have changed their benefit structure to *money purchase* (or *defined contribution* as it is usually known, more technically) – this trend being not least attributable to increased administration, cost, and future unknown liability brought about by a combination of legislation (e.g. Pensions Act 1995) and court cases (e.g. *Barber v. GRE*, and cases relating to part-timers' pension rights, including the Mrs Margorrian case).

However, in spite of this general trend it is still true to say that by far the majority of 'large' employers – both in the public and the private sectors – have pension schemes operated on the defined benefit basis. Hence, in the grid box occupational/earnings related we shall glibly enter the words 'most large schemes', acknowledging that some of these large schemes must fall elsewhere in the grid. However, it is worth noting that very few schemes with fewer than, say, 100 members are likely to offer benefits on an earnings-related basis.

Importantly for the purposes of this book, where an individual reaches retirement age within one of these schemes it is the employer, not the retiree, who is responsible for providing the retirement income and it is therefore the employer who – if he or she buys an annuity at all (they usually *don't*, preferring instead to pay retirement pensions out of their own fund on an ongoing basis) benefit from any enhanced or preferential terms made available from annuity providers (for example on the grounds of a retiree's ill health, offering an impaired life annuity).

Defined contribution
An increasing number of medium and large employers (see discussion above) and the continuing vast majority of smaller employers establishing an occupational pension scheme do so on the defined contribution basis: they know how much they are prepared to contribute to the arrangement and do not want to be committed to a particular level of retirement benefit.

Many of these schemes have only a very small number of members (often only one member) covering senior directors and executives. In this category schemes are often called *Director Pension Plans* (DPPs), *Executive Pension Plans* (EPPs), and the more specialized *Small Self-Administered Schemes* (SSASs) – the acronyms of which we shall now enter into our pensions grid.

Generally, though by no means always, used to describe slightly larger schemes (perhaps with 10 members or more, though with no upper limit) are the descriptions *Contracted Out Money Purchase Schemes* (COMPS) and *Contracted In Money Purchase Schemes* (CIMPS). In this respect, 'contracting out' refers to opting out of SERPS.

In contrast to defined benefit schemes, particularly important for the purposes of this book is the principle that the better the annuity rate that can be selected from the accumulated fund the better the retirement income for the scheme member. Against that principle, if a defined benefit scheme secures a preferential annuity rate the benefit belongs, in effect, to the scheme.

Apart from the scheme names we are entering into the appropriate grid box you should also be aware that Additional Voluntary Contributions (AVCs) and Free Standing AVCs (FSAVCs) are members of the occupational pension scheme regime, even though they might *look like* personal ('individual') pensions. Both AVCs and FSAVCs are occupational pension schemes (and therefore have benefits restricted to a proportion of the individual's final remuneration, as described in Chapter 3) but, whereas FSAVCs are *always* established on a money purchase basis (as dictated by legislation), AVCs may be offered either as money purchase (now becoming the norm) or on an *added years* basis (being earnings-related, because the scheme pays benefits as a proportion of the member's final pensionable salary). We therefore, in our grid, include FSAVCs under occupational/defined contribution and AVCs under occupational pension/defined contribution *and* occupational pension/defined benefit because the latter variation can fall within either category.

Finally, Pension Buy Out Bonds, being a vehicle that accepts transfer values from other occupational pension schemes, is itself an occupational pension scheme, technically. Moreover, it is quite a complex animal because it is usually established mostly as a defined contribution scheme, and partly (usually the lesser proportion) as a defined benefit scheme.

The pensions grid

You should be aware that the occupational pension environment is highly complex and is explained in more depth in Chapter 3. For now, however, content yourself at least to accept and understand the way in which we now make the appropriate entries into our pension grid (with only the personal pension line to complete):

Benefit Paying Method

Pensions 'pillar'	Flat Rate	Defined Benefit	Defined Contribution
State-provided	Basic state pension	SERPS	✗
Occupational	very few/e.g. industry-wide scheme for building workers	most large schemes. Very few schemes with under 200 members	Increasing number of larger schemes, but also: EPPs, DPPs, SSASs, COMPS, CIMPs (some) AVCs, (all) FSAVCs, part of pension buy out bonds
Personal	✗	✗	

PERSONAL PENSIONS

Flat rate
No personal pensions offer benefits on the *flat rate* basis

Defined benefit
No personal pensions offer benefits payable on the defined benefit basis.

It is, however, perhaps worth noting that an increasing number of employers are establishing pension schemes for their employees, or amending their existing schemes, as a group of personal pension policies. These schemes may look at first sight to be occupational pension schemes because they appear to be established and administered by the employer. However, the employer is in fact operating as little more than a conduit between each individual employee and the personal pension provider – almost invariably collecting premiums for the insurance company by deduction from the employees' wages. In the vast majority of instances the employer also makes contributions.

In a significant number of group personal pensions the employer calculates that, given a certain level of contributions (employer and/or employee) and an assumed investment growth rate on the accumulating fund, benefits payable at a member's retirement will provide, say, 50% of that person's pre-retirement income (again, making assumptions as to the member's final salary). These may appear not only to be occupational pension schemes but, more precisely, defined benefit occupational schemes. In fact, they are neither: the 'final salary' projection will almost invariably be only that – *a projection*. It is most uncommon for an employer to provide a money purchase grouped personal pension scheme and then guarantee the benefits on a defined benefits basis: after all, one of the advantages of this type of scheme, for the employer, is the avoidance of making long-term benefit promises that could in future be very expensive to secure.

Defined contribution
All personal pensions and their forerunner, retirement annuity contracts, are established on a money purchase/defined contribution basis. This means, of course, that the risks associated with investment performance and future annuity rates rest firmly and squarely with the individual pension scheme member.

Pensions grid

We can now complete the remainder of the pensions grid, referring to this (if required) over the coming couple of chapters where we look in much more detail at personal pensions and occupational pension schemes.

Benefit Paying Method

Pensions 'pillar'	Flat Rate	Defined Benefit	Defined Contribution
State-provided	Basic state pension	SERPS	✗
Occupational	Very few/e.g. industry-wide scheme for building workers	Most large schemes. Very few schemes with under 200 members	Increasing number of larger schemes, but also: EPPs, DPPs, SSASs, COMPS, CIMPs (some) AVCs, (all) FSAVCs, part of pension buy out bonds
Personal	✗	✗	Personal pension plans Retirement annuity contracts

SUMMARY

This chapter is intended only as an outline summary of the main methods by which a pension scheme may be established and how benefits accrue under those schemes. We look no further at state pensions because the individual cannot amend the annuity basis of these benefits. Over the next two chapters, however, we must investigate private sector pensions – both occupational and personal – in much more depth to ascertain certain factors and features that will affect the retirement income option decision.

2 Personal Pension Arrangements

INTRODUCTION

Many books have been written solely on the topic of personal pensions, and it would be easy to attempt in this book to include much detail of these important schemes. However, we are of course concentrating here on such detail, and only such detail, as impacts on the retirement option decisions relating to personal pensions and so we are able to omit much technical information about what does or can happen to personal pensions before retirement.

However, first of all we have felt it desirable to ensure readers have a reasonable basic understanding of these schemes and, further, we have included sufficient detail to understand a number of retirement option planning strategies discussed throughout this chapter and the remainder of the book.

In this chapter we shall be looking at the classes of pension plans that would be arranged on an individual basis and not connected in any way with an employer's pension. The plans that we shall be covering will therefore be those that would be held or arranged by persons who either are or have been in non-pensionable employment, or in self-employment. Individuals who have been employed would have come within the orbit of the State Earnings Related Pension Scheme, or SERPS, and may have taken an option on an individual basis to contract out of SERPS, and we shall cover that area of pensions as well.

It is possible for a person to be both employed and in an employers' pension scheme but have other income from another occupation that is non-pensionable employment or self-employment, and such persons may also have or could arrange the types of individual polices that we shall be looking at in respect of those additional occupations.

PERSONAL PENSIONS

A person who was in non-pensionable employment or in self-employment may have benefits that have accrued from what is known as a Personal Pension Policy, available since April 1988. There were earlier types of personal pension arrangement, which may well have been called personal, but legislatively were called Retirement Annuities. Some people coming up to retirement may have these older policies and we shall be looking at them as well later in the chapter and seeing how they differ from personal pension policies.

Background legislation
The legislation enabling personal pensions was contained in the Social Security Act 1986, but the detailed tax rules are in the Finance Act (2) 1987. The relevant taxation provisions were subsequently consolidated into Chapter IV, Part XIV of the Income and Corporation Taxes Act 1988 – often referred to as the Taxes Act.

Although personal pensions are available only to those who are self-employed or have earnings from a non-pensionable employment, the legislation does allow employers, who wish to, to contribute either on top of a member's contribution or in isolation. Some employers set up such arrangements on a group basis for more than one employee rather than the more formal alternative employers' pension scheme. A person in one of these group personal pension arrangements might actually think he was in pensionable employment as he is, on the face of it, in an 'employers' scheme', but he would not have been in what the Inland Revenue and Occupational Pensions Office recognize as 'pensionable employment' or have been in an occupational pensions scheme.

PERMITTED CONTRIBUTIONS TO PERSONAL PENSIONS

You may feel that detailed consideration of maximum allowable contributions to personal pensions is irrelevant to a study of retirement income options ('too late by that time'!). But an understanding, if not a detailed knowledge, of principles including carry forward (otherwise known as *unused relief)* is crucial to an appreciation of the important retirement planning strategy commonly known as *Immediate Vesting Annuities* under which a large single contribution may be made at, just before, or even just after retirement to secure particularly attractive additional retirement income.

Contributions may be made to personal pensions by either individuals and/or their employers. There are statutory limits regarding the maximum contributions that may be accepted by both personal pension schemes and retirement annuities (covered later in this chapter). These are expressed as a percentage of what are called by the Inland Revenue net relevant earnings.

Net relevant earnings

Net relevant earnings are defined in Section 646 of the Income and Corporation Taxes Act 1988 as relevant earnings (which excludes earned income from a job that carries pension rights) less certain deductions for business expenses including any deductions for trading losses or capital allowances that may apply to the self-employed.

MAXIMUM PERMISSIBLE CONTRIBUTIONS TO PERSONAL PENSIONS

The maximum permissible contribution for any tax year is in accordance with the table below. These maximum figures include any employers' contributions in respect of the employed:

Age at 6 April	Maximum % of Net Relevant Earnings
Up to age 35	17.5%
36-45	20%
46-50	25%
51-55	30%
56-60	35%
60+	40%

Notes
- Up to 5% of net relevant earnings (included within the above limits) may be paid towards life insurance and/or dependants' pensions as long as these benefits are payable on the member's death before age 75.
- The earnings cap introduced in the Finance Act 1989 (see below) applies to the maximum earnings in respect of which the contribution limits are used.

The earnings cap

The Finance Act 1989 introduced a top limit on the earnings that may be taken account of for the purposes of calculating maximum personal pension contributions.

The earnings cap for the 1999/2000 tax year is £90,600

The earnings cap applicable to earlier tax years, which could possibly be relevant, is shown below:

Tax Year	Earnings Cap £
1998/99	87,600
1997/98	84,000
1996/97	82,200
1995/96	78,600
1994/95	76,800
1993/94	75,000
1992/93	75,000
1991/92	71,400

UNUSED ALLOWANCES

If allowances in previous years have not been fully used, they can be used in a subsequent year, or years, using either what is known as either a carry forward provision or a carry back allowance. These are not the same and have important differences.

Carry forward
If a person was entitled to make a certain level of contribution in a particular tax year but none or only part of it was actually used, then the unused part of the year's allowance can be carried forward for up to 6 tax years.

If in a particular tax year a person wishes to use unused allowances from the previous 6 tax years, the total contributed in the tax year must not exceed the net relevant earnings in that tax year.

Before unused allowances can be used, the total allowance for the year in which the contribution is to be actually made must be used first. When all the current year's allowance has been used then and only then can unused allowances be added, starting from the earliest tax year possible for which there is an unused allowance, and then working forward.

Carry back
Carry back differs from carry forward in that, even though a contribution may be made in the current tax year, it can be treated for tax purposes as though it was actually contributed in the previous tax year. It then attracts relief against the income tax for that year and not the current year.

If an individual had no net relevant earnings for the previous tax year, the contribution can be carried back to the tax year before that but no further.

Furthermore, by making use of the carry back provision an individual can then consider using carry forward provisions for the 6 years prior to the year in which the contribution was deemed to have been made and not when actually made. This can have the effect of extending the carry forward from 6 years to either 7 or 8 years.

A person can make use of the carry back provision without having to firstly make use of the current year's allowance.

Employers' contributions

Neither the carry back nor the carry forward provisions can be used in respect of employers' contributions – only in respect of employees' contributions for earnings from employment as opposed to self-employment.

Example of carry back and carry forward

John Smith is now aged 61 (as at the beginning of the current tax year) and his net relevant earnings for the current tax year, 1999 to 2000, are £40,000. He has so far in this tax year contributed £14,000 into personal pensions, whereas his total limit is 40% of net relevant earnings or £16,000.

In previous years his contributions and net relevant earnings have been as follows:

Year	Net Relevant Earnings	Contributions Made	Contributions Allowable	Unused Balance
	£	£	£	£
1998/99	80,000	21,000	28,000 (35%)	7,000
1997/98	55,000	12,000	19,250 (35%)	7,250
1996/97	50,000	12,000	17,500 (35%)	5,500
1995/96	45,000	12,000	15,750 (35%)	3,750
1994/95	40,000	8,000	14,000 (35%)	6,000
1993/94	40,000	8,000	12,000 (30%)	4,000
1992/93	40,000	6,000	12,000 (30%)	6,000

Under the carry forward provisions John would firstly use up his unused allowance for the current tax year 1999/2000, i.e. £2,000. He would then start to mop up unused allowances going back firstly to 1993/94, the earliest year for which there are unused allowances that he can mop up within the 6-year time limit. The total unused allowances including that for the current tax year would amount to £35,500. Although John would be able to use all of that in the current tax year because the total does not exceed his net relevant earnings of £40,000, much of that contribution would be within the basic rate of income tax or even lower whereas it is advantageous for him to obtain as much relief at the higher rates that he can. Furthermore, he has not been able to mop up the unused allowance for 1992/93 because it is too far back.

Under the carry back provisions, John decides that he will firstly contribute £7,000 of his unused allowances and have it treated as though he had paid that contribution in the tax year 1998/99. He then makes use of carry forward rules for that year and starts to mop up from 1992/93 forwards. His remaining total unused allowances for the years 1992/93 to 1997/98 amount to £32,500, and he could choose to allocate that between the tax years 1999/2000 and 1998/99 to get as much as possible within those bands of income for obtaining as much tax relief as possible, rather than all against just the one year. If he wished to offset any unused allowances against the 1999/2000 tax year, he would also have to contribute the £2,000 of unused amount for that tax year before he could do so.

USE OF UNUSED ALLOWANCES

Unused allowances from personal pensions provide a valuable tool for maximising pension in retirement for those persons who are coming up to or have even retired and have the capital available to do so. It is an area that can be overlooked, especially if a person has already retired and yet is still within the time frame that would enable him or her to make use of these allowances, particularly if use can be made of the carry back provisions to a tax year when total income might have been higher and in a higher tax level. We said above how if there were not any net relevant earnings in the previous tax year, then a person could carry back to the year before that.

It is possible for a person to invest into a personal pension plan with a view to benefiting from the tax relief obtained and actually take the benefits immediately, if so desired. The attraction of this is covered in the next section.

IMMEDIATE VESTING

It is possible with a personal pension to invest a single sum and immediately take the benefits. This is a very useful option to consider for the person who has not made full use of allowances and has the capital available to be able to mop up some or all of them using the carry back and carry forward options mentioned earlier.

Just how attractive the return will be to a person depends on two factors, in particular:
- the rate of tax relief obtained upon the contribution paid,
- the rate of annuity that can be obtained for the pension fund remaining after the tax-free cash sum is taken.

Rate of relief
The person who is able to obtain tax relief at 40% on the whole of the contribution invested obviously has a much lower net cost than someone who obtains tax relief only at the basic rate of tax, or at a marginal rate between the two. The rate of relief obtained makes a significant difference to the overall rate of return.

Annuity rate
The rate of annuity is important in that a very low rate of annuity would make the rate of return look very unattractive compared to other ways in which the capital could have been invested. Broadly speaking, the rate of income after tax from the annuity has to be such that it is worthwhile giving up the capital to obtain it. If the rate of return is only slightly higher than that from an alternative investment that could produce income, or interest, without losing the right to the capital, then investing into a personal pension to vest it immediately would have little to recommend it. The younger a person is, the more likely it is that the rate of income will be unattractive.

Example of benefits
The benefits that can be provided through effecting a personal pension policy and then immediately vesting it are best shown by an example.

Example

Mr Smith, who is 65, makes a gross contribution to a personal pension of £50,000 (utilizing carry forward).

Gross Contribution	£50,000
Tax Relief	£20,000
Effective Net Contribution	£30,000
Maximum Tax-Free Cash (taken immediately)	£12,500
Effective Net Cost after return of Tax-Free Cash	£17,500
Gross Annuity (say)	£3,750 p.a.
(based on remaining fund of £37,500 after Tax-Free Cash)	
Gross return in relation to Effective Net Cost	21.43%
(i.e. £3,750 as a percentage of £17,500).	

This simplified example ignores charges levied by the annuity provider and also assumes a certain notional underlying annuity interest rate. It should, however, serve to illustrate the potential advantages of immediate vesting annuities, particularly for higher rate taxpayers – a 20%+ annual return on his investment! Note, though, that whether the annuity would continue beyond his death would depend on the annuity options selected.

Note also that this strategy is available to anyone eligible for a personal pension, beyond the age of 50, even if not retired.

WHEN BENEFITS MAY BE TAKEN

Personal pension benefits must normally be taken between the ages of 50 and 75, but with certain exceptions, for specified occupations – broadly professional sportsmen – who may take benefits from the age of 35 or 40 (depending upon the sport concerned).

Benefits may also be taken before the age of 50 on the grounds of serious ill health. For this provision to apply the individual must be permanently unable to undertake his or her normal occupation or any other occupation for which they might be suited. It is necessary that the personal pension scheme provider receives medical evidence to support the claim of incapacity. It should be noted, however, that benefits arising out of any State scheme contributions paid into an appropriate personal pension (which generate protected rights benefits), may only be taken from the age of 60 or later irrespective of the degree of incapacity.

It is particularly important to note that it is not necessary for an individual personal pension scheme member to have retired to be able to start taking the benefits from a personal pension (or, indeed, from retirement annuity contracts, which we will discuss later); it is sufficient simply for the member to have attained the age of 50 (or earlier, for certain occupations).

Moreover, when an individual *does* retire it is not necessary for him or her to start to take the benefits from the personal pension – he or she may leave the fund to continue to grow in a largely tax-exempt environment until, under current legislation, he or she is obliged to vest (start drawing) the benefits no later than age 75.

Finally, and crucial to a consideration of certain types of flexible annuity strategy (in particular *phased retirement*, as discussed in Chapter 8), it is not necessary to vest all the benefits from a personal pension at the same time; subject to the personal pension provider's scheme being established with sufficient flexibility, the scheme member may take parts of the benefit at, say, age 51 to be followed by further parts of the fund over the following years (always ensuring, of course, that all the fund is vested by age 75).

THE TYPES OF BENEFITS AVAILABLE

There are various ways in which the holder of a personal pension can choose to take the annuity using the fund that has been created. In Chapter 4, we comment upon how annuities can be taken in different frequencies, have guarantee periods, and be either on a single or joint life basis, and in addition be either level or increasing, either on a fixed basis, or linked to a company with profits or unit-linked fund.

Although all the fund can be used to provide for an annuity to be purchased, there is a valuable option in any personal pension policy, with one exception, to take part of the fund as a tax-free cash sum. As will be seen in Chapter 4, even if the policyholder would wish to have the fund to be used solely to provide income, there are tax advantages in taking any cash sum available and using that sum to purchase an annuity, a purchased life annuity, separate from the main compulsory pension one.

The tax-free cash sum

At retirement, an individual may choose to exchange part of his or her personal pension benefit for a tax-free cash sum of up to 25% of the fund value. In making this calculation, the amount of any fund arising from Department of Health and Social Security contributions, through contracting out of the State Earnings Related Pensions Scheme, must generally be excluded (i.e. in respect of Protected Rights benefits). However, if the personal pension was taken out before 27 July 1989 the fund arising out of any such contributions may be included in the tax-free cash calculation if it forms part of the same arrangement but excluding the value of widow's or dependant's benefits, which would have been included in part of the fund built up from those DHSS contributions. Later in this chapter we cover in more detail the special rules relating to the way in which benefits can be taken from a personal pension in respect of contributions from the DHSS.

Further restrictions may apply in respect of any transfer payments that have been made into a personal pension from another form of pension scheme, and these restrictions are covered below.

RESTRICTIONS ON CASH SUM FOR FUNDS ARISING FROM TRANSFERS

During a person's working lifetime, he or she may have been in different types of pension arrangement and for one reason or another decided to transfer any accumulated pension fund from those arrangements into a personal pension. Because the rules on tax-free cash sum options differ for other types of pension arrangements, there are special provisions to ensure that any fund accumulated as a result of a transfer does not enable a person to have a higher tax-free cash sum from that accumulated fund than would have been available under the origin\al pension arrangement. This is to stop people transferring funds with a view to increasing the amount of tax-free cash sum that they can take.

Free-standing additional voluntary contribution schemes
Although, for example, a transfer may be taken from a Free-Standing Additional Voluntary Contribution scheme, which is an individual top-up arrangement to an employer's occupational pension scheme, to a personal pension there is a certificate issued at the time of transfer, called a nil cash certificate. This prevents tax-free cash being taken in respect of that part of the fund that has accumulated out of such a transfer value. This is because tax-free cash is not an option under a Free-Standing AVC scheme.

Occupational pension schemes
Where benefits are transferred from an occupational pension scheme to a personal pension then in the following circumstances it is necessary for the personal pension provider to obtain a certificate from the trustees of the transferring scheme, indicating the maximum tax-free cash sum that would have applied had the transfer not taken place:
- where the transfer is in respect of a person who is, or has been during the last ten years, a controlling director or,
- where the transfer is in respect of a person whose earnings are, or have been during the last ten years, greater than the then value of the earnings cap or,
- if at the time of the transfer the person is aged 45 or more or,
- where the Inland Revenue has specially approved an earlier normal retirement date than would usually apply.

Without such a certificate no tax-free cash in respect of the transferred benefits may be taken.

Revaluation of the certified tax-free cash
In calculating the amount of tax-free cash sum that may be taken in respect of

any transfer from an occupational pension scheme when the personal pension benefits are actually taken, the certified tax-free cash figure may be increased in line with the Retail Prices Index from the date of the transfer until retirement. The tax-free cash sum that will then be available from the personal pension fund that has resulted from the transfer will be the smaller of the revalued amount or 25% of the appropriated accumulated fund. As with all personal pension funds, any part of the fund representing protected rights benefits would still have to be excluded. Protected rights are those benefits that have accrued from contributions from the Department of Health and Social Security as a result of contracting out of SERPS on an individual basis through an occupational pension scheme, or through that part of an employer's pension scheme that was segregated as being protected rights where the employer's scheme itself was contracted out of the SERPS scheme.

PENSIONS OPTIONS

Before looking in more detail as to the pension options, it is appropriate to comment now on an option known as the open market option. It does not effect the amount of tax-free cash sum that a person can take but can enable the policyholder to increase the amount of annuity available from the remaining pension fund, or alternatively be able to obtain the type of annuity that the holding company may not itself provide.

The open market option
On retirement, the personal pension planholder may transfer the accumulated value of his or her pension fund or funds to any life office or friendly society to purchase pension benefits. This allows individuals to seek out the best annuity rates available on retirement.

Alternatively, it may be that the company that has been used to accumulate the pension fund may not provide the type of annuity that the policyholder wishes to have. If, for example, the policyholder wished to have a with profits annuity but that option is not provided by the existing company, then he or she would need to transfer the fund to a company that does provide such an annuity.

TRANSFERS FROM OCCUPATIONAL PENSION SCHEMES INTO PERSONAL PENSIONS

When an individual transfers benefits from an occupational pension scheme into a personal pension, a benefits check is conducted if:
- the member has been or is a 20% controlling director in respect of the employment to which the transfer relates at any time during the period of 10 years before the date on which the right to a transfer value arose; or
- the individual's annual remuneration in respect of the employment to which the transfer relates is or was more than the allowable maximum for any year during the period of tax years before the date on which the right to a transfer value arose.

The purpose of the test, which is calculated in accordance with Retirement Benefits Schemes – Transfer Values (Evidence Note 11), is to check that the accrued benefits are not overfunded. If the benefits fail the test the transfer value cannot proceed. Therefore, if a person has a personal pension policy resulting from such a transfer the test has already been carried out and satisfied.

The reason for the test is that if it were not in place and a director was overfunded, he or she could transfer benefits into a personal pension plan where there would be no restrictions on the overall benefits that could be taken, even though there might still be restrictions on the tax-free cash sum under the various personal pension rules given earlier.

DEATH BENEFITS

With personal pensions the benefit payable on death before retirement benefits are taken would normally be a return of the value of the pension fund at the time of death, or a return of the premiums paid plus interest at a specified rate, depending upon the basis upon which the policy was provided, unless provision has been made for the benefits to be payable in the form of a pension for dependants.

On the member's death *after* retirement provision may be made for a surviving spouse's or dependant's pension to be payable from the annuity, although the level of the survivor's pension may not exceed the level of the member's maximum allowable pension. In other words, the survivor cannot be paid an income greater than the member could have enjoyed.

Dependants' benefits and transfer payments from an occupational pension scheme or a Section 32 Plan
A further issue arises where payment into the personal pension has been made arising out of a transfer payment from an occupational pension scheme or a Section 32 Plan. (A Section 32 Plan was an arrangement that enabled an employee who left an employer to transfer from the old employer's scheme into an individual arrangement rather than a new employer's scheme, should they have had a new employer. It was used more before personal pensions became available.) In this instance, a maximum of 25% of that part of the fund may be paid out as a pre-retirement death benefit, with the balance being used to provide for a dependant's pension. If there is no spouse or other dependants then the whole fund may be paid out in cash form.

RETIREMENT ANNUITIES

Before personal pensions, which were introduced from 1 July 1988, retirement annuities were the type of pension plan that the self-employed and those not in a company pension scheme used to save for their retirement. Retirement annuities could be offered only by insurance companies and friendly societies and in many ways are very similar to personal pensions. Retirement annuity plans, like personal pensions, will generally be of a type where the premiums paid build up a fund and the fund so secured is then used to provide retirement benefits. However, some of the older policies provided a specific minimum amount of annuity, which was increased by profit additions, if with profits, and if any of these older policies are coming to maturity, that minimum pension rate might well be worthwhile at a time when open market rates are at a historic low point. Benefits may be taken at any time between the ages of 60 and 75 (not 50 to 75 as with personal pensions). As with personal pensions, it is not necessary to retire in the sense of completely ceasing to work, in order to take benefits.

The rules applicable to personal pensions grew out of those that evolved over many years in respect of retirement annuities. So it is not surprising that in some instances, as will be covered later in this chapter, the rules that apply to both personal pensions and retirement annuities are the same.

The differences between personal pensions and retirement annuities will be highlighted when appropriate but unless such a mention is made, it can be taken that the same rules apply as given earlier for personal pensions.

Background legislation

The legislation governing retirement annuities was contained in Section 226 of the Income and Corporation Taxes Act 1970 and as subsequently amended. The relevant legislation is now contained in Chapter III Part XIV of the Income and Corporation Taxes Act 1988.

Retirement annuity contracts were thus granted approval by the Inland Revenue under Section 620, Chapter III Part XIV of the Income and Corporation Taxes Act 1988 and approval could be granted only to contracts offered by life insurance companies and friendly societies. To be approved the retirement annuity could not be capable of being surrendered for cash, and it must not be possible for the retirement annuity to be assigned to a third party.

MAXIMUM PERMISSIBLE CONTRIBUTIONS TO RETIREMENT ANNUITIES

The maximum permissible contributions that may be made into existing retirement annuity contracts are based on an individual's age as at the 6 April, as in the following table:

Age at 6 April	Maximum % of Net Relevant Earnings
Up to age 50	17.5%
51-55	20%
56-60	22.5%
60+	27.5%

Earnings cap

The earnings cap that applies to personal pensions does not apply to retirement annuities unless a contribution is being made into a personal pension in the same tax year. This has implications if there is an intention to contribute into a pension plan in the tax year because the lower percentage limit for retirement annuities could be offset by the lack of the earnings cap.

Example:

If Mr Jones is aged 55 and has net relevant earnings of £150,000 he could only invest 30% of only £90,600 into a personal pension, i.e. £27,180. However, he could invest 20% of the whole £150,000 into a retirement annuity, £30,000, provided that he had an existing retirement annuity that could take additional contributions. He could not start a new one.

ELIGIBILITY TO CONTRIBUTE TO A RETIREMENT ANNUITY CONTRACT

Retirement annuities are allowed to receive contributions only from the holder of the plan and so the plans cannot be used to contract out of SERPS. The retirement annuity may not accept employer contributions, which means that if an employer did pay in to an employee's retirement annuity, these payments would have to be taxed on the employee as if they were in the form of remuneration. The employee would then claim income tax relief on that contribution in the usual way.

BENEFITS FROM RETIREMENT ANNUITY CONTRACTS

Benefits from a retirement annuity may comprise:
- A pension for the member and perhaps his or her dependants or
- A tax-free cash sum of up to three times the pension that remains after the tax-free cash has been taken.

The tax-free cash calculation from a retirement annuity

The above statement is in reality the end result of a calculation, where the starting point is the calculation of the maximum residual pension. Three times the maximum residual pension gives us amount of the maximum tax-free cash sum from a retirement annuity. It is therefore not as simple as with a personal pension where one can take 25% of the cash fund accumulated.

Calculation of the tax-free cash

The following formula can help in calculating the maximum tax-free cash sum:

$$\text{Reduced pension} = \frac{\text{Pension before tax-free cash is taken}}{1 + (\text{three times annuity factor})}$$

The annuity factor or annuity rate is based on the cost of buying a single life level pension, with no guarantee, payable annually in arrears.

The residual pension, although it is calculated based on a single life, non-escalating annuity that is payable annually in arrears with no guarantee, the actual annuity can actually be purchased in a different format, as with a personal pension.

Although an open market option is available, use of the option would involve transferring the fund into a personal pension unless the individual had a number of retirement annuity policies and was able to make a transfer into one of them. The personal pension rules on tax-free cash limits would then apply, which could have a detrimental effect on the amount of tax-free cash that can be taken, despite giving a potentially higher annuity rate.

Which gives the highest tax-free cash sum?

An interesting exercise is to use the above formula to calculate the annuity rate at which the maximum retirement annuity tax-free cash sum is equal to the 25% of the fund maximum tax-free cash sum applicable to a personal pension. This occurs at an annuity rate of 11.11%.

This means that at an annuity rate of less than 11.11%, payable annually in arrears, on a single life basis, with no guarantee, a greater tax-free cash sum is available from a personal pension. And at an annuity rate of more than 11.11% a greater tax-free cash sum is available from a retirement annuity. The annuity rate for this calculation is the cost of buying a single life level pension, payable annually in arrears, non-escalating and with no guaranteed minimum period.

This can well be a factor to take into account as regards how best to use funds to top up pension provision using unused allowances. It may or may not be advantageous to make additional contributions to a retirement annuity should the existing policy be able to accept one as an alternative to contributing to a personal pension policy.

It is possible to transfer an accumulated fund from a retirement annuity policy to a personal pension policy, which a person might consider doing should either the tax-free cash sum available be greater or benefits be required between the ages of 50 and 60. It is not, however, possible to transfer from a personal pension to a retirement annuity.

STATE PENSIONS AND CONTRACTING OUT

1988 also saw the introduction of appropriate personal pensions (APP), that is an arrangement in the ownership of the individual that is able to accept rebates of Class 1 National Insurance Contributions from the Department of Social Security as an alternative to accruing benefits within the State Earnings Related Pension Scheme.

This meant that employees who were participating in the State Earnings Related Pension Scheme, and were not already contracted out through membership of a 'contracted out' occupational pension scheme, were able to use a personal pension policy to contract out of SERPS.

Rebates of National Insurance contributions into approved personal pensions give rise to protected rights benefits, and from a personal pension scheme these protected rights benefits can be taken from age 60 or later but must be taken by age 75 at the latest.

The following sections of this chapter advise on the special provisions relating to approved personal pensions and protected rights.

APPROPRIATE PERSONAL PENSIONS

A personal pension scheme used for this purpose is known as an appropriate personal pension. Because an approved personal pension may also receive additional contributions from the employee and/or the employer as well as transfer values from other personal pensions, retirement annuities, and occupational pension schemes, when a person comes to take benefits from a policy that has received such additional contributions, the pension providing company needs to ensure that the special provisions relating to protected rights are followed.

Changing providers

If an individual wished to use a different pension provider for receiving contracted out rebates subsequent to the original decision, he or she could do so. Completing the forms for the new provider caused the Department of Health and Social Security to send subsequent payments to the new company. A person can therefore have more than one approved personal pension policy.

If he or she so wished, a person could transfer an accrued pension fund, including any protected rights, from one provider to another.

PROTECTED RIGHTS

The benefits provided out of National Insurance rebates are known as protected rights. The fund arising out of those contributions are known as the protected rights fund and must be used to provide for pension benefits on a prescribed basis. It must be possible for these benefits to be purchased on the open market, and they may be paid monthly, or at longer intervals.

A special provision that does not apply to ordinary personal pensions is that the pension purchased from the protected rights fund has to be purchased at unisex and unistatus annuity rates. By this is meant that the annuity rates used are the same for males and females. For those who are single when the protected rights annuity is purchased, there is a requirement in respect of the amount of fund arising from rights purchased for the period up to the end of the 1996/97 tax year for provision to be made for a spouse's pension, but for rights purchased from 6 April 1997 there is no such requirement.

Furthermore, up to 1996/97 the period of contracting out through a personal pension resulted in the calculation of a notional guaranteed minimum pension (GMP), which was deducted from the SERPS benefit that would otherwise have applied, and the state provided for any inflation-proofing of this notional GMP on the excess over 3% per annum. However, no such provision applies in respect of the protected rights purchased by contributions after 6 April 1997.

Restrictions applicable to protected rights

Because protected rights have been purchased through the investment of rebates from the Department of Health and Social Security, there are restrictions on how benefits are taken using the protected rights fund. These are:

- The protected rights element must be taken in the form of a pension from age 60 and before the age of 75 with no tax-free cash sum allowed. However, in respect of arrangements set up between 1 July 1988 and 26 July 1989, the value of the protected rights fund may be taken account of in calculating the 25% of fund value that may be taken from the excess over the protected rights fund if the policyholder or his or her employer had been making additional contributions into the same plan, because those additional contributions do provide for a tax-free cash sum option entitlement.
- Unisex/Unistatus annuity rates must be used. This means that the same annuity rates are used for both males and females. If the member is married when the benefits are purchased provision must be made for a spouse's pension benefit but if single then only the rights purchased before 6 April 1997 have to be used to provide for a spouse's pension benefit.

- Up until April 1997 it was obligatory that a dependant's pension to a qualifying spouse or other dependent must be provided following the member's death if there is one. This is no longer a requirement.
- In the event of death before state pension age then, if there is no qualifying spouse (see below), the funds accumulated within the protected rights fund may be paid out as a lump sum, but where there is a qualifying spouse then a pension must be purchased for that qualifying spouse.
- All pensions purchased out of the protected rights fund must increase in payment by a specified amount or the rate of increase in Retail Prices Index (RPI), if lower. The protected rights benefits purchased arising from rebates in respect of the 1997/8 tax year onwards will be required to increase by 5% per annum or the rate of increase in RPI, if lower. Those rights benefits arising from rebates from earlier tax years will need to be increased in payment by only 3% per annum or the rate of increase in RPI, if lower.

Protected rights and income withdrawal

It has been permitted with effect from April 1996 for the facility known as income withdrawal (described fully in Chapter 8) to be applied to the protected rights benefits. The tables for this purpose to be prepared by the Government Actuary's Department will be based on joint life annuity rates and will be the same for males and females. Where the member has died, then in respect of the surviving spouse single life rates will be used as the basis.

The annuity rate basis underlying the tables will be based on benefits that are indexed in payment to reflect the provisions applicable to protected rights benefits when they are purchased outright. In this regard the level of indexation applicable adopted in the basis underlying the tables will reflect 3% indexation on the protected rights accrued prior to 6 April 1997 and 5% indexation on the protected rights accruing after 6 April 1997.

Trivial benefits

As from 6 April 1996 the Pensions Schemes Office has allowed the personal pension fund to be paid as a lump sum where the pension payable would be trivial in amount. The requirements to be satisfied for this purpose are:

- The fund may be paid to the member so long as (where protected rights benefits are involved) the member is aged 60 or over.
- Where protected rights are not involved then the member must be aged 50 or over or be retiring on the grounds of ill health.
- The total pension fund before any tax-free cash sum is taken may not exceed either £2,500 or the amount required to purchase an annuity of £260 per annum.
- That part of the amount paid that is in excess of the usually calculated tax-free cash sum is taxable in the tax year of payment.
- The member must not be in receipt of income withdrawals from the arrangement.
- The member may not also be a member of another personal pension.

DEATH BENEFITS FROM PROTECTED RIGHTS

We commented above regarding the special provisions relating to payments applicable on death of the policyholder. The provisions relating to death differ depending upon whether death occurs before or after taking the pension benefits.

Death before taking pension benefits

The protected rights fund must be used to purchase benefits for a qualifying spouse or other dependent. If there is no qualifying spouse or other dependants, then the cash value of the protected clients fund must be paid either to the member's estate or for the benefit of nominated beneficiaries. A qualifying spouse is a surviving spouse (that is a widow or widower) who is at the date of the protected rights member's death either:

- Aged 45 or more or
- Under age 45 with one or more dependent children, where a dependent child is defined as a child where there is entitlement to child benefit.

A dependent may otherwise be someone who is financially dependent on the member.

Payment of spouse's pension

A spouse's annuity must be paid to the qualifying spouse at least until he or she either:
- Dies or
- Remarries before state pension age or
- While under the age of 45, ceases to reside with a child under the age of 16 or to be entitled to child benefit in respect of a child under the age of 18.

This is the minimum requirement to be contained in the personal pension provisions and the personal pension of a particular provider may provide for the protected rights pension to be paid throughout the lifetime of the qualifying spouse. The spouse's pension may be guaranteed for a period of up to 5 years from its commencement date.

Any further continuation of pension benefits following the death of a qualifying spouse may, however, only be for the benefit of any children for whom the spouse immediately before death was entitled to child benefit and only so long as at least one child is under the age of 18. This continued pension must not be greater than that which would have been payable to the spouse had he or she survived.

The spouse's protected rights pension in payment must increase annually in accordance with RPI, to a maximum of 3% or 5% per annum.

Commutation of spouse's pension

Where the total value of the protected rights spouse's pension is under £260 per annum then it may be fully commuted for cash so long as the personal pension scheme arrangement rules have been amended as permitted by Statutory Instrument 1990/1142 and so long as all of any non-protected rights benefits under the scheme are being paid as a lump sum, because there is no spouse's pension payable.

Death of the member after taking pension benefits

The provisions again depend upon the existence or otherwise of a qualifying spouse or of another dependent. If there is a qualifying spouse or other dependent following the individual's death, a pension at the rate of at least 50% of the member's protected rights pension continues to be paid.

Qualifying spouse

The qualifying conditions in relation to a qualifying spouse are the same as applicable to death before state pension age, and the spouse's protected rights pension must as a minimum continue in payment until the spouse either dies, or remarries while under state pension age, or while under the age of 45 ceases to reside with a child under the age of 16 or ceases to be entitled to child benefit for a child under 18. Once again, the pension provider's own policy wording may provide for the pension to continue to be paid through the qualifying spouse's lifetime.

Although the qualifying spouse's pension must be at least 50% of the rate of the member's continuing pension had he or she survived, it may be at anything up to the full rate of the member's pension during the balance of any period not exceeding 5 years following the commencement of payment of the member's pension. In other words, providers have the option to allow a 5-year guarantee period on the member's pension from the protected rights fund, payable to a qualifying spouse in place of a 50% spouse's annuity, for that period.

No qualifying spouse

If there is no qualifying spouse, the personal pension scheme rules may permit the protected rights pension to be paid instead to a non-qualifying spouse or to any other dependants. A dependent other than a child must be demonstrably financially dependent upon the member. Such a pension on the individual concerned must cease on his or her becoming financially independent. Where there is no qualifying spouse or other dependant, then the protected rights pension benefits may be paid for any children in respect of whom the member immediately before death was entitled to child benefits. This may remain in payment only for so long as at least one of the children is under the age of 18.

In the above situation, the pension paid must not be greater than 50% of the member's own pension prior to death, except that once again, using the pension guarantee option, the pension payable for the balance of any period not exceeding 5 years following the commencement of the member's pension may be anything up to the full rate of the member's pension.

Pensions in payment under these provisions must again be increased annually.

PROTECTED RIGHTS BENEFITS AND GUARANTEES

Benefits provided through protected rights do not have to secure a minimum benefit. If the protected rights benefits provide for a benefit lower than what the State Earnings Related Pension Scheme would have provided, that was at the risk of the individual and the state will not make up any shortfall.

Conversely, if the protected rights benefits so purchased exceed those that would have come from SERPS, the individual benefits accordingly.

3 Occupational Pension Schemes

INTRODUCTION

In the previous chapter the options at retirement in respect of personal pension arrangements were covered. In this chapter we look at the options available to persons retiring who have benefits arising from pension arrangements provided by their employer through schemes recognized as occupational pension schemes.

These will also include additional methods available to members of such schemes for enhancing their retirement income which involved making additional contributions into arrangements that were either into the employer's own additional voluntary contributions arrangements or into free-standing additional voluntary contribution plans arranged individually by the employee.

The special provisions relating to benefits arising from schemes that contracted their employees out of the State Earnings Related Pension Scheme will also be covered.

Occupational pension schemes are constrained by the maximum benefits framework laid down by the Pension Schemes Office (PSO) to be able to receive and retain the tax benefits of being approved by the PSO as what are known as exempt approved schemes. A scheme approved under these rules does not necessarily have to provide the maximum benefits allowed under the rules, but cannot provide *more*.

This point is perhaps the most important issue to understand in reading this chapter: through careful selection and management of certain retirement income options it may be possible to significantly enhance the benefits payable to the pension scheme member and/or his or her spouse and dependants. However, if that enhancement takes the possible benefits above the limits imposed by the Inland Revenue then the enhancement cannot be paid in full;

the member may never be paid more than the Inland Revenue limits, even if he or she has sufficient funds to otherwise make this possible.

NORMAL RETIREMENT AGE

An approved scheme will have a normal retirement age that reflects the age at which an employee is actually expected to retire. This must now be the same for males and females and equal treatment must be given in respect of benefits accrued after 17 May 1990. The permitted range for the normal retirement age is for males and females is 60 –75. However, an earlier normal retirement age may be approved at the discretion of the PSO for certain occupations, but there is not, contrary to popular belief, a list of approved earlier normal retirement ages as with personal pensions.

FINAL REMUNERATION

Allowable benefits from occupational pension schemes are based upon final remuneration.

There are two possible definitions of final remuneration, which are:
- The remuneration received in respect of any one of the 5 years before normal retirement age. Any fluctuating earnings to be averaged over 3 or more consecutive years.
- The average of total earnings received in any period of 3 or more consecutive years that end not more than 10 years before normal retirement date. Note that remuneration earned but not actually received by the member may be included so long as any such remuneration is actually paid within 3 years of retirement. The averaging process applies to such remuneration.

Where during or after the 1987/88 tax year final remuneration exceeds £100,000 or if the member is or has been in the 10 years prior to retirement a controlling director, the second of the above definitions must be used.

Additional special provisions apply in relation to controlling directors, which will be considered further later.

Benefits in kind

In calculating final remuneration, taxable benefits in kind, for example the assessable value for tax purposes of a company car, may be taken into account. Profit-related pay may be included as a part of pensionable remuneration so long as it is treated as fluctuating earnings and is thus averaged over 3 or more consecutive years. Earnings in respect of any year before the last year may be increased by the Retail Prices Index to normal retirement date. This process is often referred to as dynamization.

MAXIMUM BENEFIT LIMITS

Under the rules for pension scheme approval there are basic maximum benefits that will be automatically allowable under a scheme, and then beyond that special provisions relating to those employees who have less than 40 years of service.

Basic pension benefits

Basic pension benefits comprise one-sixtieth of final remuneration for each year of service with the employer, subject to a maximum of 40 years to count. It is the period of service with the employer that is relevant – not just the years of membership of the scheme.

The maximum allowed pension benefit from the scheme is forty-sixtieths or two-thirds of final remuneration. This is a benefit that can always be provided and without any reference to what are called retained benefits from any previous schemes. **In Appendices 1, 2, and 3 we shall be covering the effect of retained benefits that have to be taken into account where an employee is being provided with a rate of benefit greater than the basic 1/60th of salary for each year of service.** This means that where just basic pension benefit limits are provided, any benefits from other schemes in which the member may have previously participated may be ignored, as can any earlier benefits from retirement annuities or personal pensions.

So the maximum pension for someone with 40 years service to normal retirement date will be 40/60ths or 2/3rds of final pay plus retained benefits **(see Appendix 3)** and with no overall maximum. The only limitation on this will be a limit on the salary that forms the basis of the calculation known as the earnings cap.

Example

Jane was employed as a senior manager with a multinational company earning a salary of £80,000. At the age of 52 she accepted early retirement terms and took an immediate pension of £35,000 p.a. Jane did not wish to stop working and joined a local firm of house builders as a sales consultant with a salary made up of basic salary plus commission. She joined their final salary scheme which provided a pension of one sixtieth of earnings for each year of service at a normal retirement age of 60.

Jane is now 60 so has completed 8 years of service with her new employer. Her final salary is £20,000, including £5,000 of commission. Pensionable salary under the rules of the scheme is basic pay and takes no account of any bonuses. She is therefore able to have a pension of eight sixtieths of £15,000, or £2,000 per annum without having to take into account the retained benefit represented by the pension in payment of £35,000 p.a.

Basic tax-free cash benefits

The basic maximum tax-free cash sum is 3/80ths of final remuneration (already defined above), in respect of each year of service with a maximum of 40 years to count. So the maximum permissible tax-free cash benefit according to this formula is 1.5 x final remuneration. This basis is sometimes referred to as the 3n/80ths scale.

Under this basis any cash benefit arising from schemes of which the individual may have previously been a member may also be ignored.

The only limit that will apply will be if the salary that can form the basis of the calculation is limited by the earnings cap.

The tax-free cash sum is provided from the scheme by giving up part of the scheme pension — it is not additional to it.

EARNINGS CAP

The 1989 Finance Act introduced the earnings cap where earnings in excess of the level of the cap are ignored for the purposes of calculating maximum benefits. The cap was originally set at £60,000, and has been adjusted from time to time to reflect inflation. Currently, it is £90,600. This earnings cap applies to any approved pension scheme irrespective of length of service where the scheme was set up on or after 14 March 1989 or the member joined a scheme on or after 1 June 1989 where the scheme was set up prior to 14 March 1989.

SERVICE OF LESS THAN 40 YEARS

Many people will be unable to complete 40 years service with the same employer, and thus given the strict interpretation of the basic pension benefits limit rule will be unable to earn a full two-thirds of final salary pension. Under discretionary approved schemes, which represent the majority, an employer is able to enhance the benefits, potentially up to the 2/3rds limit for those members who will have less than 40 years of service by the scheme normal retirement date – possibly for those with as few as 10 years' service.

The detailed rules relating to this enhancement are frequently complex. Much depends on the date the pension scheme was originally established and/or the date on which the individual member joined that scheme. It is, however, crucial for retirees to be able to ascertain the maximum permissible benefits in these circumstances to establish the maximum level of pension benefits – both at the date of retirement and beyond – allowed by the Inland Revenue.

For members of a scheme with defined benefits, the benefits provided are limited by the employer, and yet the Inland Revenue limit may allow higher benefits. This can be relevant if a transfer to an individual pension arrangement was being considered because it could be that the transfer value might purchase higher benefits on the open market than those that would be provided from the scheme. Another class of retiree for whom the complex rules could be appropriate is the person who was in a money purchase scheme, rather than a defined benefits scheme, because the fund accumulated needs to be used to its maximum extent.

The author strongly suggests that retirees to whom this *accelerated accrual* may be applicable (occupational scheme members with less than 40 years' service) should obtain an actuarial assessment of the relevant maxima – both pension and tax-free cash – before any consideration of the different retirement options available.

The full rules are set out in Appendix 1 at the back of the book.

INCREASES OF PENSION BENEFITS IN PAYMENT

Any pension benefit being paid may always be increased to the maximum permissible level applicable at the date of retirement or death as appropriate.

In addition, the maximum approvable pension may be increased in line with the Retail Prices Index or 3% if greater, calculated from the date at which the benefit was first payable.

At retirement the pension may be set up to provide a rate of increase in anticipation of increases that may be desirable in the future. Where an annuity is purchased at retirement, for example, because the annuity will tend to be one that either provides for increases at a fixed rate, or one that is linked to returns obtained under a pension provider's with profits or unit-linked fund, it may well happen that the rate of increase in any one year would take the total income provided to an amount that is greater than the Inland Revenue would allow. In periods of high inflation, this tended not to occur. However, in recent times inflation levels have been very low, and even zero or negative inflation is a possibility that might have to be considered.

Therefore, although the pension company itself has the necessary funds to pay a particular level of pension, or has contracted to do so when the annuity was first purchased at retirement, it could have to limit the amount of annuity in a particular year to ensure that the average rate of increase since the pension started to be paid did not exceed either 3% per annum or the actual rate of increase in the Retail Prices Index, if greater.

With a unit-linked or unitized with profits annuity, all that would happen is that the pension provider would cash only the number of units necessary to provide the allowable income for the year, and the units that did not need to be cashed would be left to accumulate in value to enhance the prospects for the income to increase in future years.

With a pension that was intended to increase at a fixed rate greater than 3% per annum, any increase that could not be paid would have to be retained with the pension company, as a credit for any subsequent year when the average rate of inflation had risen to enable it to be paid.

TRIVIAL BENEFITS

Where the value of pensions payable to an employee from his employer are less than £260 per annum, the entire pension benefits may be exchanged for a lump sum benefit. Tax at 20% will be charged on the excess over the maximum tax-free cash sum normally available.

LATE RETIREMENT

In respect of service after normal retirement date, benefits may be increased in accordance with the following rules.

Less than 40 years' service
Where service at normal retirement date is below 40 years, further years of service toward calculating maximum basic benefits may be granted but not so as to exceed the maximum period of service that would have been achieved had the date of actual retirement been the normal retirement date. For example, if an individual had achieved 38 years service to his or her scheme's normal retirement date, then despite working for an additional five years, maximum benefits could only be based upon 40 years, so allowing a pension of 2/3rds of final pay.

More than 40 years' service

Where service at normal retirement date is greater than 40 years and where the 1989 Finance Act rules either do not apply or have not been adopted in respect of the member, an additional sixtieth of final remuneration may be earned in respect of each year of service after normal retirement date so long as an overall maximum of 45/60ths of final remuneration is not exceeded.

As an alternative to the relevant approach above, the benefits that applied at normal retirement date may be increased to take account of cost-of-living increases during the time of post-normal retirement date service, or if greater, the increase in benefit determined by the scheme actuary so as to reflect the increase in the actuarial value of the benefits in respect of the period of late retirement.

For post-1989 regime members, no additional benefits are allowed to be provided for service completed after normal retirement date where 40 or more years have been completed, beyond the maximum approvable benefits allowed at normal retirement date excepting any increases to compensate for inflation or to reflect the fact that the pension will be paid for a shorter period.

Tax-free cash and late retirement

Similar provisions to the above apply in relation to the maximum tax-free cash sum. So where service at normal retirement date is greater than 40 years, and where the 1989 Finance Act rules either do not apply or have not been adopted, each additional years service may provide for an additional tax-free lump sum benefit of 3/80ths of final salary subject to an overall limit of 135/80ths.

EARLY RETIREMENT

In general terms scheme members leaving after the age of 50 may take an immediate pension if they wish, part of which they may exchange for a tax-free cash sum.

Under the early retirement rules the basic scale for both pension and tax-free cash benefits already referred to (that is n/60ths and 3n/80ths respectively) are available based on service to the date of early retirement and with no restriction in relation to any retained benefits **(See Appendix 3)** which may therefore be added, provided the basic scale benefits are not exceeded.

If benefits are to be enhanced using accelerated factors, then as with normal retirement, the maximum benefits that can be taken depend upon the regime applicable for the member.

As with benefits at normal retirement for members with less than 40 years of service, the Inland Revenue rules are extremely complex. If relevant to a retiree, they are extremely important.

The full rules are set out in Appendix 2 at the back of the book.

EARLY RETIREMENT ON THE GROUNDS OF ILL-HEALTH

If an individual is forced to retire through ill-health, the maximum benefits payable are those that would have been payable at normal retirement date, based upon final remuneration at the date of early retirement. For these purposes, ill-health means that the individual must be so incapacitated as to prevent him or her from pursuing normal employment or at the very least to seriously impair earning capacity.

It is very likely in these circumstances that the employee has less than 40 years of service. If, however, he or she could have completed 40 years of service by normal retirement date, then Inland Revenue rules on the maximum benefits relating to that number of years would be applied. It is more likely, however, that the employee could not have completed 40 years of service by normal retirement date and in that case the comments made above in respect of normal retirement with service of less than 40 years apply. Again, it is the years that could have been completed by normal retirement date and not those actually worked that apply in this circumstance.

In exceptional circumstances of serious ill-health where it can be demonstrated that life expectancy is so short (that is, less than 12 months) as to make it unreasonable for benefits to be taken in pension form, then it can be possible for the early retirement pension to be commuted for a cash sum.

The element of the lump sum payment which represents pension which otherwise would not have been commutable for cash is taxable at a rate of 20%.

SPECIAL RULES FOR CONTROLLING DIRECTORS

The possible definitions of a controlling director depend upon the date on which the member joined the pension scheme. Generally a director is regarded as being a controlling director if at any time after the 16 March 1987 and within 10 years of leaving the scheme he or she was a director and owned, alone or with associates, or was able to control directly or indirectly, 20% or more of the ordinary share capital of the company.

An associate for this purpose means:

- A relative or partner.
- The trustees of any settlement where the director has transferred shares in the company.

Where the director is a pre-1987 member he or she is regarded as being a controlling director if at that time he or she was a director who, either alone or together with his or her spouse and minor children, was or became the beneficial owner of shares which, when added to any shares held by the trustees of any settlement into which the director or his/her spouse transferred assets, carried more than 20% of the voting rights in the company providing the pension or in a company controlling that company.

Restrictions applicable to controlling directors

Benefits of all controlling directors must be based on the definition of final remuneration requiring an averaging of earnings over 3 or more consecutive years except with regard to the calculation of death benefits, where the additional permissible definitions of final salary already referred to may be taken account of. Certain other conditions also apply including:

- Where the controlling director is a pre-1987 or a 1987 to 1989 member, then when calculating maximum pension entitlements, benefits from retirement annuity policies and personal pensions must

- be taken into account even where the benefit provided is not greater than straight 60ths in respect of each year of service, so that the total benefit provided does not exceed 2/3rds of final pay.
- A similar restriction applies to the calculation of the maximum tax-free cash sum for controlling directors.
- In the event of death in service after the age of 75 it would not normally be allowed to have a discretionary disposal of death benefit for the avoidance of inheritance tax purposes.
- If benefits are deferred after normal retirement date, maximum benefits will be calculated on the basis that the date when benefits are actually taken is the normal retirement date. Subsequent Retail Price Index-based increases are, however, allowed.
- If the member is able to take the tax-free cash sum at normal retirement date and the pension is deferred, normal retirement date is taken as the date on which the tax-free cash sum is taken with the maximum pension calculated as at that date. This amount may, however, be subsequently increased with reference to Retail Prices Index for the period of deferment.

ADDED BENEFITS

Very few people are able to be in a position to achieve 40 years service with one employer and thus achieve maximum benefits even under a final salary scheme unless their employer is prepared to make some augmentation to their benefits. It is, however, possible for an employee in an employer's pension scheme to augment his or her pension with the taxation advantages that arise from pension arrangements. An employee who is in an employer's pension scheme cannot effect an individual personal pension but is, however, still able to augment his or her employer's normal pension scheme benefits. This can either be through what is known as additional voluntary contributions or alternatively free-standing additional voluntary contributions.

Additional voluntary contributions
All employers who provide an occupational pension scheme must also provide

for an employee to 'top up' benefits by making additional contributions into the pension scheme and these contributions are called additional voluntary contributions or AVCs.

The employee may contribute up to 15% of his or her remuneration to an AVC, although this maximum is reduced by the amount of any contribution he or she is making into the main occupational scheme.

This maximum amount may be reduced still further if it is likely that the benefits purchased together with the benefits from the main scheme will provide total benefits in excess of Inland Revenue limits.

The benefits from contributing to an employer's AVC scheme can be provided in one of two ways:

- Some occupational pension schemes allow the employee to buy what is known as added years. The employee agrees to pay a certain percentage of salary into buying one or more added years and his length of membership in the scheme is then artificially extended.
- Most schemes have the AVC contributions being at a level determined by the employee in that they will provide eventual benefits solely based on the investment growth on those contributions within the employer's scheme.

There is not any provision for carry back or carry forward as there is with personal pensions. If, therefore, an employee is coming up to retirement and has not taken any significant steps by way of AVCs to maximize possible pension, there is little that he or she can do at retirement, which will have a significant effect on overall income, in the way that he or she could have done with a personal pension, particularly if unable to immediately have part of the AVC cost returned as tax-free cash. If, however, the employer's scheme is one that works on added years, the purchase of added years close to retirement, if allowable, might be worthwhile, because the additional benefits produced are not dependant upon investment growth. This can be particularly useful if the employee has had a salary increase of a significant amount, depending upon the cost of the added years.

Example

Mr Jones has 15 years of service and his salary up until a year before retirement was £15,000. He had a salary increase 12 months prior to retirement to make his salary £20,000. He has been advised that the cost of buying an added year is 5% of salary. His scheme provides a pension based on 60ths.

If he did not buy an added year his pension entitlement would be 15/60ths of £20,000 or £5,000.

If he bought an added year for a cost of £1,000 (5% of £20,000), his pension entitlement would be immediately increased by 1/60 of £20,000 or £333.33 per annum gross.

If a 25% taxpayer this would net down to £249.98 per annum, but his net cost would have netted down to £750. This means that within just over 3 years he would have had the full return of his cost.

Tax-free cash
No part of the benefits purchased from AVC contributions can be taken in cash apart from those arrangements started before 8 April 1987.

However, where an employee started contributing into an AVC arrangement before 8 April 1987, the fund that accumulates from those contributions – including those still being made under the pre-April 1987 commitment – may be taken in part as a tax-free cash sum within the overall tax-free cash sum rules.

Benefit options
As with the main pension scheme, the way in which benefits are provided at retirement is determined by the employer. Therefore, whether pensions increase in payment and any level of spouse's pensions will be as per the main scheme.

Free-standing AVCs
Free-standing AVCs are stand-alone pension arrangements provided by pension providers and are attractive to many employees who desire more control over the investment strategy of their voluntary contributions, or who wish to have flexibility of the options for taking benefits and not be governed by the options provided under the employer scheme.

The maximum contributions are the same as for employer's own AVC schemes but benefits are always dependent upon investment growth. The comments made with regard to added years do not therefore apply to free-standing AVCs. As with AVCs there are not any provisions for carry back or carry forward.

Multiple FSAVCs
Although it is not possible to contribute to more than one FSAVC in any one tax year, an employee has been able to contribute to a different provider in one tax year to that in a previous year. Furthermore, even if an employee is contributing to his employer's AVC arrangement, he or she is still allowed, subject to overall limits, to contribute into a separate FSAVC.

Also, if an employee with a free-standing AVC changed employers, even if he or she continued with the same pension provider, a separate arrangement had to be set up in respect of the new employment.

This means that an employee could have more than one free-standing AVC policy and in addition also have benefits from an employer's in house AVC scheme.

Benefits from free-standing AVCs
Benefits that accrue within an FSAVC will relate to the investment returns on those contributions. If the accumulated fund produces benefits which together with the benefits from the main occupational scheme causes Revenue limits to be exceeded, then the excess fund must be returned to the employee and this excess will then be subject to a tax charge.

This tax charge will be at the rate of 33% for a basic-rate taxpayer at that time or 47.79% if he or she is a higher rate taxpayer.

No tax-free cash can be taken from a free-standing AVC arrangement.

Benefit options
The employee can chose at retirement to have his or her pension increase or not increase irrespective of the provisions of the main scheme in this respect. Furthermore, he or she can also choose whether the benefits from the AVC will incorporate any spouse's pension and the level of this irrespective of the provisions of the main scheme.

OCCUPATIONAL PENSIONS SCHEMES AND THE STATE EARNINGS RELATED PENSION SCHEME

If an employer's approved pension scheme was used as a vehicle for contracting employees out of the State Earnings Related Pension Scheme, the employee would not have had an individual choice. He may have noticed or been advised that, as a result, the amount of National Insurance that his employer deducted from his salary reduced. Unlike personal pensions where the National Insurance was paid in full, and the Department of Health and Social Security transferred money to the pension, with an occupational pension scheme it was the employer who remitted contributions to the pension provider.

There are certain provisions with regard to benefits that apply in respect of contracted-out schemes and these are outlined below. Inherently, there are two main types of employer's scheme. There are those that provided defined benefits and guaranteed so many 60ths or other chosen fraction of final salary in relation to years of service, called defined benefit schemes, and those that built up a fund and the eventual benefits would reflect the value of the fund at the time of retirement and prevailing annuity rates with a provision that benefits actually provided could not exceed approvable pension scheme limits, and such arrangements are called money purchase schemes.

DEFINED BENEFIT SCHEMES

Originally there were benefit requirements imposed on defined benefit schemes that in practical terms resulted in the contracted-out scheme more than replacing the SERPS benefit foregone as a consequence of contracting out through the requisite benefits test. Then from 1986, it was a requirement that contracted-out schemes providing defined benefits satisfied a test known as the guaranteed minimum pension (GMP) test. This test was replaced in respect of members contracted out of defined benefit schemes for benefits earned from April 1997 by what became called requisite benefits requirements, which meant that the concept of a GMP will disappear as time goes on, but still applies for people retiring in the foreseeable future for the period of contracted-out membership of the scheme between 1986 and 1997.

The guaranteed minimum pension (GMP)

Where a scheme was contracted out under the GMP test then a guaranteed minimum pension had to be forthcoming from the occupational pension scheme which, broadly speaking, represented at least what membership of SERPS would have provided during the period of contracted-out employment had the employee been contracted in.

An occupational pension scheme that was contracted out under the GMP test also has to provide for a guaranteed minimum spouse's pension of at least 50% of the member's GMP entitlement, and from the 1988/89 tax year this was extended to encompass a widower's pension. The SERPS benefit eventually received by the member would then be reduced by the value of this notional GMP.

GMPs ceased to accrue after 6 April 1997.

Protecting the value of the GMP

Up until 6 April 1988, inflation-proofing of the GMP in line with the movement in the RPI was provided by the Department of Social Security. In relation to any GMP accruing within the scheme from 6 April 1988 the occupational pension scheme must inflation-proof that part of the GMP accruing from 6 April 1988 by up to 3% per annum with any further inflation-proofing required to maintain the real value of the GMP being met by the DSS.

The position after April 1997

For the contracted-out member from 6 April 1997 no longer is there a reduction in SERPS by a notional GMP value. The benefit from the contracted-out scheme is, from 6 April 1997, a straight replacement for the SERPS benefit foregone.

Previously members of contracted-out schemes accrued SERPS benefits which were reduced by the amount of GMP payable. After 5 April 1997 this changed, and a member of a scheme contracted out on the new basis will not accrue any further SERPS benefits.

MONEY PURCHASE OCCUPATIONAL PENSION SCHEMES

From 6 April 1988 it became possible for occupational pension schemes that were based upon a defined contribution or money purchase formula to contract out. These schemes became known as contracted out money purchase schemes (COMPS). Under these schemes there was not any requirement to include a benefit guarantee.

In the same way as with approved personal pensions, covered in Chapter 2, an employee who was contracted out through a COMP could end up with either more or less than the benefit he or she would have received having remained in the State Earnings Related Pension Scheme, depending upon the investment performance of the pension company and annuity rates prevailing at the time pension benefits are taken.

Protected rights

In the same way as approved personal pensions, the benefits provided by the amount of contributions that reflected the National Insurance contribution reduction produced a fund known as protected rights, and certain conditions attach as to how the benefits can be provided by that fund, as compared to any additional benefits secured by employee or employer normal contributions.

The protected rights fund must be used to provide for pension benefits on a prescribed basis as with personal pensions. So in summary:
- The pension purchased from the protected rights fund of a COMPS must be purchased at age 60 or later up and by the age of 75, and must provide for a pension bought on unisex/unistatus annuity rates.
- The protected rights element must be taken in the form of pension with no tax-free cash sum allowed.
- Unisex/Unistatus annuity rates apply, meaning that the pension must be purchased at the same price for males and females irrespective of sex and subject to the division between pre-April 1997 protected rights

and post-April 1997 protected rights the rates used must be the same irrespective of marital status.
- In respect of the pre-April 1997 protected rights fund there must be a spouse's pension purchased following death before or after retirement. Before retirement (again in respect of pre-April 1997 protected rights) the protected rights fund must be used to provide for a spouse's pension benefit on the member's death before retirement, and when the member's pension is purchased at retirement a 50% spouse's pension following the member's death must be included. However from April 1997 it has become possible for a single man at retirement to opt for the purchase of a single life pension, but unisex annuity rates will still apply. This provision applies only to the protected rights fund from post-6 April 1997 contributions.
- The annuity purchased must be increased in payment by the lower of the rate of increase in Retail Price Index or a fixed amount. For the protected rights fund pre-April 1997 this fixed amount is 3% per annum. For the protected rights fund from post-6 April 1997 contributions rebates in respect of tax year 1997/98 onwards the rate of escalation will be the lower of the rate on increase in Retail Price Index or 5% per annum. This provision applies also to any spouse's pension purchased.
- From 5 April 1997 the relationship with the SERPS benefit ceased. No longer in respect of the post-5 April 1997 period will there be a notional GMP by which SERPS will be reduced. Benefits provided through protected rights do not have to secure a minimum benefit in the nature of the guaranteed minimum pension. If the protected rights benefits provide for a benefit lower than what SERPS would have provided, that is the risk of the individual and the state will not make up any shortfall. However, if the protected rights benefits purchased exceed those that would have come from SERPS, the individual benefits accordingly.

SUMMARY: PERSONAL AND OCCUPATIONAL PENSIONS

Having defined the restrictions on the contributions or benefits (as appropriate) for personal and occupational pensions, it is now feasible for us to examine, throughout the remainder of the book, the various annuity options available to individuals seeking to take benefits from one or more of the schemes we have discussed.

You should be particularly aware of the benefit restrictions detailed or highlighted over the last couple of chapters, not least because any attempt to exceed these limits by clever selection of annuity options (including various flexibility options) will usually end in failure: it might *appear* that enhanced retirement income may be secured (say, depending on impressive fund growth in an investment-linked annuity option) but if these enhancements exceed any relevant Inland Revenue benefit limits the retiree may never see the benefits!

4 Basis of Conventional Annuities

INTRODUCTION

All pension plans, whether arranged on a personal basis or through an employer, have one thing in common. At the time the benefits from the scheme come to be taken, the plan will provide for some or all of those benefits to be taken as an *income*. The term used for this income is an *annuity*. Although the name suggests payments are made annually, payment of income can be made at more frequent intervals during the year: typically half-yearly, quarterly, or monthly.

In this chapter we shall be giving a brief outline of different types of annuity and how they are treated for tax purposes.

For the purposes of looking at retirement income we can say that a person receives an annuity payment either from some type of pre-planned pension arrangement through an employer (an occupational pension scheme) or through plans organized by himself or herself (personal pension plans). Alternatively, he or she may use capital to purchase an annuity before, at or during retirement (a purchased life annuity).

Definition: Annuitant
The person upon whose life the payment of the annuity is dependent and whose age determines the rate of income.

THE ANNUITY BASIS

The various bases on which an annuity can be written on are:
- Payment frequency
- In advance or in arrears

- Immediate or deferred
- With or without proportion
- Payments guaranteed for a minimum period and the death benefit basis during the guaranteed period
- Single life or joint life with spouse's/dependant's benefit
- With or without overlap
- Capital protected
- Lifetime or temporary
- Level annuity or escalating.

We shall consider each one of these features in detail and how they affect the annuity rate by looking at specific quotations.

PAYMENT FREQUENCY

An individual can choose how often he or she wishes to receive a pension. The options available are monthly, quarterly, half-yearly or annually. The most common option is monthly.

Once clients have decided on how often they require the income to be paid they then have to decide between having the pension payable in arrears or in advance.

The difference the mode of payment has on the annuity rate if payments are in arrears for a male aged 62 would be as follows:

- Monthly to quarterly   + 1.0%
- Monthly to half yearly + 2.3%
- Monthly to yearly   + 5.0%

On the annuity quotation it will show under frequency of payment how the annuity is to be paid.

IN ADVANCE OR IN ARREARS

When an annuity is arranged there is normally an option as to whether it is to be paid in advance or in arrears.

If it is *in advance*, the first instalment is paid at the beginning of a period (e.g. monthly, annually etc.) and at the beginning of each subsequent period.

If *in arrears*, the first instalment is paid at the end of a period.

Example

An annuity is payable monthly in advance. The first monthly instalment is due on the day of actual purchase and thereafter at monthly intervals, which means that the second payment is made one month after the date of purchase. If the annuity is payable monthly in arrears, the first payment is due one month from the date of purchase and thereafter at monthly intervals.

If a client decided to take a pension that was payable monthly in advance and wanted to know the effect of having the annuity paid in arrears, the annuity rate would increase by slightly less than 1% but the client has forsaken a monthly payment and therefore may be out of pocket. For this reason the most common option is monthly in advance.

The highest annuity rate can be secured by having the pension paid annually in arrears because the client would have to wait for one year after the commencement date before the first payment was received. Conversely the lowest annuity rate is obtained by having a pension that is paid yearly in advance.

IMMEDIATE OR DEFERRED

This distinction dictates whether the annuity payments at the time the annuity is arranged are to commence straight away or are to be delayed for more than one year. If the income payments are due to start within one year, it would be considered to be an immediate annuity, whereas if due to start at a date which is more than one year ahead, it would be considered to be a deferred annuity.

Definition: immediate annuity

An annuity arrangement under which the first payment of income will be made within one year of the 'purchase' of the annuity. This 'purchase'

Basis of Conventional Annuities

may be using an individual's 'free' capital at the time or making use of an accumulated pension fund from either a personal or company pension arrangement.

Definition: deferred annuity

An annuity arrangement under which the first payment of income is not due until more than one year after the 'purchase' of the annuity. The start date of the income might be a fixed date, or a range of dates. Deferred annuities may be provided by means of an initial capital sum purchase, or by means of regular payments for an agreed term (as for example, monthly premiums to a personal pension).

For most people who are retiring the income would normally be provided on an immediate basis. Generally, if there was not an immediate need for additional income, and the retiring person had a choice as to whether he or she wanted to take an annuity at the time, then the 'purchase' of any annuity would normally be left until the income was needed. Although the purchase of the annuity is deferred until a later date, it is not as such a deferred annuity, because a deferred annuity is one where the 'purchase' is made and the basis of the annuity agreed at a time more than a year before the income is due to start.

As outlined in Chapter 3 an individual may not have the choice of deferring taking an annuity where, for example, his retirement date is fixed by the rules of his employees scheme.

WITH OR WITHOUT PROPORTION

If an annuitant dies part way through an annuity payment period then, depending upon whether the annuity is payable monthly or quarterly, half-yearly or yearly, there may be just a few days or as much as almost a year before the next instalment would have been paid.

Example

If an annuity is payable in yearly instalments and the annuitant dies 11 months after the previous payment, he or she would have been

63

almost due for another payment. If the annuity is arranged on a *with proportion* basis the annuity company would pay 11/12ths of the annuity payment due, whereas if *without proportion*, it would not.

This generally makes little difference to the rate of income provided by an annuity, especially where the instalments are monthly.

PAYMENTS GUARANTEED FOR A MINIMUM PERIOD

An individual can have the pension payable for life or guaranteed number of years if greater. If no guarantee period is chosen then the pension would cease on death and the quotation would read under members pension guarantee that the member's pension is payable for life.

An individual can have a pension that will have a guaranteed payment period of up to 10 years. The pension will be payable for the individual's life or if greater the guaranteed period.

The most common options are guaranteed for 5 or 10 years.

So if an individual took out a contract that was guaranteed for 5 years and then died after the second year, the payments would be guaranteed for a further 3 years so that 5 years' pension would have been payable in total.

If the pension has a guaranteed period there are various options as to how the future guaranteed payments will be paid on death during the guaranteed period. The options are:

- Continues in payment.
- Discounted lump sum.
- Undiscounted lump sum with no escalation.
- Undiscounted lump sum with escalation.

If the pension is to continue in payment and the pension is £1,000 per annum and guaranteed for 5 years' the annuity would continue until the end of the 5-year period and then cease. The wording on the quotation would be:

The member's pension is payable for life and will be paid for a minimum period of 5 years. Should the member die within this period, the pension will continue to be paid by regular instalments until the end of the guaranteed period is reached.

Alternatively the value of the unpaid pension can be paid as a lump sum and discounted to allow for early payment. So in our example if the annuity was £1,000 per annum and was guaranteed for 5 years, and the individual died after 2 years, the value of the remaining annuity instalments would be paid as a lump sum which would be reduced to allow for early payment. The lump sum payable would be in the region of £2,700 which, if then invested, could provide an income of £1,000 for 3 years when the interest is added from the investment. Whether it will be sufficient to do this will depend upon the prevailing interest rates. The wording on the quotation would read:

The member's pension is payable for life and will be guaranteed for a minimum of 5 years. Should the member die within this period, the balance of the unpaid pension to the end of the guarantee period will be paid out as a lump sum reduced to allow for early payment.

Undiscounted lump sum with no escalation. If this option is chosen the pension is not reduced for early payment and therefore, in the example we have been using, the amount payable would be £3,000. The wording on the quotation would read:

The member's pension is payable for life and will be paid for a minimum of 5 years. Should the member die within this period, the balance of the unpaid pension to the end of the guarantee period will be paid out as a lump sum.

However, if the annuity was escalating – that is, it increased during payment – then the lump sum payable may or may not take into account any future increases in the pension depending upon the rules of the scheme. The wording on the quotation would be:

The member's pension is payable for life and will be paid for a minimum of 5 years. Should the member die within this period, the balance of the unpaid pension to the end of the guarantee period will be paid out as a lump sum allowing (not allowing) for future increases that would have been paid.

If an individual decides to have a guaranteed period of greater than 5 years, then due to Inland Revenue rules he or she can only have continued payments and does not have the option of a discounted or undiscounted lump sum payable on death (IR12:12.9-12.10 and IR76 7:10-7.11).

How the remainder of the pension payments is to be paid on death during the guarantee period has very little effect on the annuity rate.

Example

The difference in rates between 5- and 10-year guarantee period increases with age as is shown in the following table.

Age	55	60	65	70	75
Nil Guarantee	100%	100%	100%	100%	100%
5 Years	99%	98%	97%	96%	94%
10 Years	98%	96%	95%	87%	83%

The reason it is more expensive for a 75-year-old man to have a guarantee period is because his life expectancy is less than for a male aged 60 and therefore there is a greater chance that he will die during the guaranteed period.

SINGLE LIFE OR JOINT LIFE

If a person is married, there is a possibility that he or she would wish the annuity income to continue to be paid after their death to the surviving spouse, if he or she predeceases the spouse. Most employers' pension schemes can be expected to have such a provision but for personal pensions the annuitant will have the choice of including such a provision.

The normal options are for the annuity to continue in full, or reduce to one-half, one-third or two-thirds of the level that applied while both parties were alive. In the next section we show the effects of the different bases on the starting level of income but, briefly, provision for annuity income to continue to be paid to a surviving spouse will result in a lower level of income than for a 'single life' annuity.

SPOUSE'S PENSION BENEFIT

In Chapter 2 we stated that the spouse's pension can be no greater than the individual's pension under a personal pension or retirement annuity contract. However, for an occupational pension scheme it cannot be greater than 2/3rds of the annuitant's maximum approvable pension. Typically the amount of the spouse's pension is 2/3rds or 1/2 of the member's pension. Again under an occupational pension scheme the benefits will match the preceding scheme.

Example
The following table shows how the provision of a spouse's pension affects the annuity rate; the spouse is assumed to be 3 years younger:

Age	55	60	65	70	75
Single life	£4,515	£4,874	£5,374	£6,123	£7,230
50% widows	94%	92%	90%	87%	84%
66.67% widows	92%	89%	87%	84%	80%
100% widows	89%	86%	82%	78%	73%

In the following section we comment upon how a spouse's/dependant's pension can be provided on a variety of bases.

SPOUSE'S/DEPENDANT'S BENEFITS

If a spouse's or dependant's pension is provided then the basis of that pension can be paid in a variety or ways, these being:
- Spouse at retirement
- Spouse at date of death single now
- Spouse at date of death married now
- Named legal dependent.

Spouse at retirement

This means the provision of a spouse's pension to the annuitant's wife or husband at the date of retirement. The wording on the quotation next to definition of spouse would be:

The spouse's pension is payable to the spouse identified above only.

Therefore if the annuitant subsequently remarried the new spouse would not be entitled to the spouse's pension.

Spouse at date of death single now

If an individual when effecting the contract is single but sometime in the future gets married, then if this option is taken the spouse at the date of death would be paid the pension. The wording on the quotation would read:

The spouse's pension is payable to the person who is the spouse of the member at the time of the member's death.

No date of birth will be shown for the spouse.

Spouse at date of death married now

If an individual when effecting the contract is married but subsequently remarries in the future, the spouse at date of death would receive the pension. The wording on the quotation reads:

The spouse's pension is payable to the person who is the spouse of the member at the time of the member's death.

A date of birth will be shown on the quotation for the current spouse.

Named legal dependant

A dependant's pension can be provided to an individual so long as he or she is legally dependent upon that individual. This could include a common-law wife and may also include a partner of the same sex as the individual.

The named legal dependent would have to be named at the outset of the contract. The wording on the quotation would read:

The spouse's pension is payable to the named dependant identified above only.

The crucial topic of definition of spouse, including the potential for providing a survivor's pension (on the death of the annuitant) for someone other than a spouse (for example a common-law partner or a same-sex partner) is considered in more depth in Chapter 5.

WITH OR WITHOUT OVERLAP

If an individual has a guaranteed payment period and has also made provision for a spouse's pension, the spouse's pension can commence on death or at the end of the guarantee period.

If the contract is guaranteed for 5 years and the member dies after 2 years, the payments can either commence on death or after the expiry of the guaranteed period. If the spouse's pension commences on death this is *with overlap* because the spouse's pension overlaps the guaranteed period. The wording on the quotation would read as follows:

The spouse's pension will commence on the day following the death of the member.

With overlap can only be added to annuities with guaranteed periods of 5 years and not 10 years (IR12 12:10)

If the spouse's pension would not commence until the expiry of the guaranteed period, this is *without overlap*. The wording on the quotation will read:

The spouse's pension will commence the day following the expiry of the guaranteed period.

The difference in rates between with and without overlap is slightly less than 1%, with the better rate being provided without overlap.

CAPITAL PROTECTED

An alternative way of ensuring that the early death does not result in the loss of the bulk of the capital used to obtain the annuity is to elect for the annuity to be *capital protected*.

Example:

Mr Jones has obtained an annuity in return for a capital sum of £50,000. He has elected for the annuity to be arranged on a capital protected basis and the gross annuity is, say, £2,500 per annum. It is paid net of basic rate income tax and he actually receives £2,200 per annum. He dies after 4 payments have been made.

The total gross payments made amount to £10,000 and therefore the balance of the cost would be paid to his estate. This would be £40,000 (£50,000 less £10,000).

It should be noted that it is the gross annuity and not the net annuity after deduction of tax that has to be used in the calculation of the capital return.

This provision would not normally apply to annuities obtained as a result of a company or personal pension arrangement but is an option where an individual's 'free' capital is used to buy the annuity.

An annuity would not include both a capital protection and a guarantee provision because they both aim to achieve the same objective but in different ways – namely that, one way or another, there will be a worthwhile return obtained in return for the capital or fund used to purchase the annuity.

LIFETIME OR TEMPORARY

When an annuity is arranged, it can either be payable for a person's lifetime or for a fixed or maximum period of years.

Lifetime annuity

This pays the annual income for the remainder of the annuitant's life, however long that might be. Even if the annuitant survives only one day after making the investment to purchase the annuity, no further income will be paid (unless a guarantee period as described earlier has been included in the annuity arrangement). The insurance company will, in costing these policies, pay regard to the mortality tables showing the life expectancy of annuitant buyers at a given age. The shorter the life expectancy the shorter the likely period of time over which the insurer will have to make annuity payments and therefore the greater will be the level of those payments.

For pension purposes, it is invariably required that an annuity is payable for life.

Temporary annuities
These pay the annual income for a specified number of years, or until earlier death, at the end of which there is no further income payable and no return of capital. Each payment therefore represents in part the income or profit on the original investment plus a return of the initial capital.

Certain 'combination' investment plans provide for a level of income for a fixed term of years with provision for return of the original investment at the end of the income term, the return of capital being provided by using part of the annuity income to fund a regular savings plan over the fixed period. Such a temporary arrangement, depending upon the rate being provided and the security of the capital return vehicle, might well be attractive to someone who is retiring.

ESCALATION RATES

If this option is chosen the pensions will increase while in payment. The escalation rate can be at a fixed rate per annum or can be in line with the Retail Price Index.

Example
The following table illustrates the reduction in the level pension if various escalation rates are added.

Age	55	60	65	70	75
Level	100%	100%	100%	100%	100%
3.0%	75%	77%	80%	82%	87%
5.0%	60%	63%	67%	71%	75%
8.5%	38%	43%	48%	54%	61%

As discussed in Chapter 3 there is a maximum limit that the pension from an occupational pension scheme can increase by, and that is that the pension will not at any time exceed the maximum approvable pension increased in line with the Retail Price Index or 3% per annum compound if greater. Therefore the pension will be monitored to ensure that Inland Revenue limits are not exceeded at some future date.

In determining the attractions or otherwise of an escalating pension for a retiree one should ascertain the 'cross over period', being the number of years the annuitant would have to survive before the income from the escalating pension equalled the (initially much higher) income for the level pension.

Example
A level pension is offered to a 65-year-old male at, say £10,000 per annum against a pension of £6,700 per annum escalating at 5%. It can be calculated that the escalating pension will not rise to £10,000 per annum until year eight.

Moreover, it should be remembered that, even at the time the escalating pension can match the level pension, the annuitant has already been foregoing considerable amounts of income and must survive many years thereafter to make up for this 'lost' money.

Much will depend on the state of health of the annuitant(s): those in poor health, with a shorter life expectancy than the national average, will usually be ill-advised to consider an escalating pension.

MORTALITY

When an individual retires at his or her chosen retirement age the life office's actuary will calculate the expected number of years the individual is expected to survive.

Example
The following table shows the life expectancy for single males and females subject to the average mortality experience of England and Wales.

BASIS OF CONVENTIONAL ANNUITIES

Age	Males Expectancy	Females Expectancy
60	16.383	20.890
61	15.681	20.093
62	14.995	19.307
63	14.326	18.530
64	13.672	17.765
65	13.036	17.010
66	12.417	16.266
67	11.815	15.533
68	11.232	14.813
69	10.668	14.106
70	10.123	13.414
71	9.597	12.737
72	9.092	12.077
73	8.607	11.435
74	8.143	10.811
75	7.699	10.207

So for a male retiring at age 60 his future life expectancy will be 16.3 years, compared to a male retiring at 65 whose life expectancy will be 13 years. Therefore, because the life office will be expecting to pay the pension for a greater number of years for a male aged 60 the cost of providing £1 of income will be higher than for a male aged 65.

The table also shows that life expectancy for females is greater than for males and therefore the cost of providing an income in retirement for a female is more expensive than for a male. The life expectancy of a 60-year-old female is 20.8 years and for a female aged 65 is 17.0 years. Compared to the life expectancy of males, the life office would therefore anticipate paying the income for a longer period of time which results in a lower level of income being provided for the same purchase price and basis.

Annuity providers will regularly monitor their annuity portfolio with regard to the actual mortality experience compared to their initial assumptions when calculating the annuity rates and will make periodic adjustments to reflect their actual experience. Mortality tables exist also for joint life expectancy an extract of which is shown below.

Age of Man	60	65	70	75
Age of Woman				
60	13.22	11.12	9.01	7.08
65	11.89	10.23	8.46	6.75
70	10.23	9.02	7.66	6.25
75	8.36	7.57	6.61	5.56

The table shows the joint life expectancy of two people (a man and a woman) of various combinations of ages, subject to the average mortality experience of England and Wales. The columns show the period for which both lives may expect to survive on average and which ends on the death of the first of the two to die.

GILT YIELDS

Once the actuary has taken into account the mortality risk he or she needs to decide what annuity interest rate needs to be used when calculating the amount of income that would be payable. To do this the actuary will look at the current yields available on long-dated gilts, that is over 15 years, before setting the annuity rate.

If we combine mortality and annuity interest rate we can show the cost of buying £1.00 of pension for different ages and interest rates. The table assumes mortality experience in line with PA(90).

BASIS OF CONVENTIONAL ANNUITIES

Exact Age	50	55	60	65	70	75
Interest						
0%	26.062	21.806	18.012	14.593	11.563	8.958
1%	22.504	19.190	16.139	13.299	10.705	8.413
2%	19.652	17.040	14.563	12.186	9.951	7.925
3%	17.340	15.258	13.227	11.222	9.286	7.486
4%	15.446	13.767	12.087	10.383	8.695	7.089
5%	13.877	12.508	11.107	9.649	8.169	6.730
6%	12.565	11.437	10.258	9.002	7.698	6.403
7%	11.457	10.520	9.519	8.430	7.275	6.106
8%	10.515	9.727	8.872	7.922	6.894	5.834
9%	9.706	9.038	8.301	7.468	6.549	5.584
10%	9.006	8.435	7.796	7.061	6.236	5.355
11%	8.397	7.905	7.347	6.694	5.950	5.143
12%	7.862	7.435	6.945	6.363	5.689	4.948
13%	7.391	7.017	6.584	6.062	5.450	4.767
14%	6.973	6.643	6.258	5.789	5.230	4.599
15%	6.599	6.307	5.963	5.539	5.028	4.443

Inflation-linked annuities

Where payments from an annuity escalate by the future rate of inflation the annuity provider's actuary must, in determining the initial rate, attempt to estimate future levels of inflation. If the actuary thinks these are likely to be very high, he or she is likely set the initial payment level very low (in anticipation of having to pay high future increases) with, of course, the reverse being true if the rate of inflation is expected to remain low. The strategy will tend to be driven by the rates of return available on long-dated index-linked gilts (as opposed to fixed-interest gilts, as discussed above, for non-inflation linked annuities), but the principles are in any case very similar.

WITH PROFITS AND UNIT-LINKED ANNUITIES

As an alternative to having an annuity that is at a fixed rate, albeit at an increasing rate rather than level, there is a desire by some annuitants to have the basis of the annuity linked to the performance of an insurance company investment fund. This can either be a 'with profits' fund or any of the other investment fund links that the insurance company provides. The annuity will hopefully rise over the years at a rate that will reflect the higher rates of return that are generally obtained from equity-related investment rather than from gilts, but obviously, there is the prospect that the annuity can fall as well as rise.

Because this alternative is a modern development that has become more attractive in recent times, we discuss it in depth in Chapter 6. A brief outline to illustrate the difference to a standard annuity is however given below.

With profits annuities
As with a standard annuity, there is a starting level of income depending upon age, sex, and any guarantees etc. that are being included. However, any provision for the income to increase in future years will be dependent upon future investment returns from the with profits fund of the annuity company. The starting rate of income is usually lower than from a standard annuity although at the time of writing, the difference is not so large as it use to be, for various reasons.

Unit-linked annuities
Under a unit-linked annuity, income in future years is directly dependent upon the investment returns obtained from a chosen investment fund, or funds. A certain number of units are purchased in the fund when the annuity is arranged and a set number will be cashed each time an annuity payment is due. The value of the encashed units will determine the level of income paid at the time. The income instalments may therefore go down as well as up but, over the long term, the annuity purchaser would expect a rising income, not least to offset effects of inflation.

EXPENSES

Expenses are obviously incurred in the initial selling of the contract and there are ongoing administration expenses over the term of the contract which need to be taken into account when calculating the income that will be provided to a policyholder. A level of expenses is therefore taken into account when calculating the annuity factor.

COMPETITION

If a life office wants to attract annuity business it has to make sure that it is offering competitive annuity rates, otherwise it will not receive any new business. Consequently the life office will collate information on current annuity rates being offered in the marketplace to ascertain its current market position.

Due to the annuity market being primarily market-rate driven – that is the best annuity rate will attract the most business – if a life office wants to attract large volumes of new business it has to ensure that it is offering competitive rates within the marketplace.

ACTUAL LEVEL OF INCOME

All the above factors when taken into account will determine the eventual level of income an individual will receive and/or their spouse for the remainder of their life.

SUB-STANDARD LIVES

When an actuary is calculating the annuity rate he or she is basing the assumptions on average life expectancy and there will be individuals who will purchase a pension annuity whose actual life expectancy will be more. There will also be individuals because of their state of health or lifestyle who will have a reduced life expectancy and a market has developed that offers enhanced rates for people with certain conditions.

Types of conditions

To qualify for what is termed an impaired annuity the individual will need to have a medical history of one or more of the following conditions:
- Obesity
- Heart attack
- Stroke
- Diabetes mellitus
- Chronic asthma
- Cancer
- Kidney failure.

Individuals who have been smoking for 10 years or more and are smoking at least 10 cigarettes a day can also qualify for enhanced terms.

These types of annuities are subject to underwriting to confirm the individual's medical history and therefore medical evidence will be obtained.

Amount of enhancement

Obviously the amount of enhancement will be dependent on the severity and type of the medical condition and which office is being used. The increase in the annuity rate is however in the range of 10% to 20% above the office's standard annuity rates.

In all other respects these annuities are the same as conventional annuities with the options available to the individual.

PURCHASED OR COMPULSORY

The tax treatment of annuity income is dependent upon where the money to purchase the annuity came from.

Compulsory purchase annuity

As the title suggests, the annuitant has no choice as to how to use the capital available. It has to be used to purchase an annuity. This would be the case in respect of the accumulated fund from a pension fund, after the tax-free cash sum (if any) had been taken (assuming any was). The remaining fund has to be used to buy an annuity and the income so obtained is treated for income tax purposes as earned income.

This means that if, when the annuity income is taken into account, the annuitant is a non-taxpayer he or she receives the income without any income tax liability. If a taxpayer, then the rate of income tax will be dependent upon the level of total taxable income, including these annuity payments. The logic behind fully taxing the income from these compulsory purchase annuities is based upon tax relief having been granted upon contributions to the pension arrangement in the past – matched by the income from the arrangement thereby being taxable.

Purchased life annuities

Where the capital used to buy the annuity did not come directly from a pension fund, part of the income will be treated as a return of the annuitant's own capital (*the capital element*) and be received free of liability to tax, and only the balance (*the interest element*) will be taxed as savings income.

Capital content of purchased life annuities

With a temporary annuity the capital content is simple to calculate. It is the capital investment divided by the term of the annuity.

> *Example:*
>
> Mr Smith has purchased a 10-year temporary annuity for a purchase price of £10,000 and receives an annuity of £1,400 per annum. The capital content of each payment is £1,000 (£10,000 divided by ten). The balance of the annuity income of £400 (£1,400 less £1,000) is the interest element.

With lifetime annuities, the term is unknown. The Inland Revenue defines the capital content as being the purchase price of the annuity divided by the life expectancy of the annuitant as indicated by mortality tables.

Example:
Consider an investment of £100,000 with the investor's future life expectancy as indicated by mortality tables being 20 years.

In this example the Inland Revenue estimates that the investor's £100,000 initial investment will be returned over 20 years and so will deem the capital content of this annuity as being £5,000 per annum. If, say, the total the annuity is £8,000 then £5,000 of that income will be represented by the capital content and be exempt from tax, whereas the balance of £3,000 will be the interest element and be liable to tax.

PURCHASED LIFE ANNUITIES AND PENSIONS

We have said above how with a compulsory purchase annuity, the whole of the annuity is taxable. Although a pension fund must generally be used to purchase an annuity, if there is provision for part of the fund to be taken as tax-free cash then it will usually be advisable to take the maximum allowable tax-free cash sum even if the retiring scheme member requires the maximum level of income.

The tax-free cash sum so taken could then be used to purchase an annuity. Although the cash came from a pension fund, the annuity purchased would not be treated as a compulsory purchase annuity because the person could, if he or she so wished, have spent the cash sum in some other way. The annuity purchased with the cash sum would, therefore, be treated for income tax purposes as a purchased life annuity and as a result benefit from the more favourable tax treatment in respect of having a tax-free capital element. A higher level of net income, after tax, is obtained compared to taking the annuity from the pension fund directly.

Example
Bill is retiring at the age of 65 and has a fund value of £100,000 from his personal pension plan.

He has decided that he requires a single life pension payable monthly, non-guaranteed and escalating at 3% per annum. He does not require the tax-free cash because he wants to maximize his income in retirement and believes that the return he will get on the tax-free lump sum would not be as great from the pension annuity.

The fund value of £100,000 would provide a gross income of £8,595.20 per annum. Let us assume that Bill's income is such that with the income from his pension, he is a basic-rate taxpayer. This means that the income of £8,595.20 will be taxed at 23% (the then current basic rate). The net annuity payable will therefore be £6,274.49 per annum.

However, if we look at the alternative to taking all the fund built up as pension, and instead have Bill make use of his tax-free cash sum option, a different net income results.

The tax-free cash would be £25,000, which when applied to a purchased life annuity would provide a gross annuity of £1970.76 per annum. The capital element of this would be £1019.11, leaving a taxable interest element of £951.65. Tax on that interest element at 23% would be £218.88, which when deducted from the gross annuity of £1970.11 leaves a resulting net purchased life annuity of £1751.88 per annum.

The remaining pension fund of £75,000 would still have to provide a compulsory purchased annuity. The gross annuity from that would be £6446.40, which after tax at 23%, would result in a net income of £4834.80 per annum.

Taking the two annuities combined, Bill's total net income would be £6586.68 (£1751.88 plus £4834.80) as compared to that of £6274.49 if the whole fund of £100,000 had been used to provide a compulsory purchase annuity.

Bill will therefore be provided with an increase in net income of £312.19 per annum, which represents an increase of just under 5%.

This principle applies to all personal pension and retirement annuities and also occupational money purchase pension arrangements (see Chapter 3) but not necessarily to defined benefit ('final salary') schemes (although even here, a comparison may identify a similar benefit).

SUMMARY

In this chapter we have summarized many of the factors that determine the level of annuity that will be obtained in relation to capital applied in its purchase. The reader will have seen how many choices are involved when a person requires to have an income provided through an annuity arrangement.

We have also shown how the tax treatment of an annuity is dependent upon the source of the capital involved in its purchase.

In the next two chapters we cover in greater depth two of the factors that need to be explored more fully – namely provision for a spouse and the ability to have the level of annuity payment increases directly linked to insurance company funds.

5 Definition of Spouse and Dependant

INTRODUCTION

In this chapter we shall examine the circumstances under which a pension may be paid, following the death of an annuitant, to a surviving spouse or some other person.

The important issues discussed here, building on the brief outline in section 4 (definition of spouse), affects benefits from occupational pension schemes as well as annuities bought from an insurance company.

An understanding of the concepts and detail is crucial for anyone comparing the relative advantages of conventional annuities with any of the flexible annuity options. It is also crucial in understanding the circumstances in which a transfer from an occupational scheme to an alternative annuity option (be it conventional or flexible) may be extremely beneficial for the retirement income of the scheme member.

WHEN IS A SPOUSE NOT A SPOUSE?

The answer to this question, within the context of pension scheme members, has an important impact as regards payment (or, more pertinently, non-payment) of a dependant's pension benefits and is not as simple as a member might think.

Frequently, in pension schemes, there is provision for a pension to be payable to one or more dependants of a deceased scheme member. The definition of dependant varies, however, between schemes and can cause undue and unfulfilled expectation that benefits may be paid to one or more persons who fall outside the definition used by a particular scheme or annuity-providing insurance company. This chapter identifies the main differences and highlights the financial planning issues arising from each definition.

FINAL SALARY AND MONEY PURCHASE PENSION SCHEMES

In final salary pension schemes there will almost invariably be provision for a pension to be payable to a surviving spouse of a deceased scheme member, whether that member dies before or after retirement. There will also usually be provision for further pension benefits to be paid to any dependent children of the deceased member, although these pensions will frequently be at a lower level than that payable to the spouse.

The main issues in this respect involve identifying the spouse entitled to receive the pension on the death of the member (not as easy as it may sound) and identifying whether a dependant's pension may be payable, on the death of a member, to his or her common-law spouse or, indeed, to a same-sex partner.

These generous provisions for spouses and dependent children are not so frequently found guaranteed in occupational money purchase schemes nor, it could be argued, in personal pensions (although certainly in the latter case the full value of the deceased's fund becomes payable as a tax-free lump sum benefit if death occurs before annuity benefits are purchased). However, in all cases (except unfunded schemes, and within flexible annuity arrangements before age 75) the money purchase fund must be used to buy an annuity, at retirement, payable for the lifetime of the pension scheme member. This annuity may or may not include provision for all or part of the member's pension to continue to be paid to a spouse (usually) or other dependant (less frequently). Here again it is vital to identify the definition of spouse or dependant used by the annuity provider.

Providers of pension annuities – primarily for money purchase schemes – invariably offer purchasers the option of having the pension ceasing on the death of the member, or continuing thereafter, in full or part, to a nominated 'second life' – usually, of course, a spouse. If such continuation is selected at outset a lower pension is payable to the scheme member because the provider may anticipate the likelihood of having to continue pension payments beyond the death of the member. Commonly known as joint life pensions' (a misnomer, it may be noted) it is, for similar reasons to those outlined for final salary schemes, important for an adviser and his or her client to identify whether a surviving spouse's pension (if selected) would be paid to the spouse at date of retirement (i.e. the date of annuity purchase) or to the spouse (if any) at date of death.

LEGALLY MARRIED SPOUSES – MARRIED AT WHAT POINT IN TIME?

On the face of it there should be little argument as to the legitimacy of a claim by a legally married spouse to be paid benefits from a pension scheme which makes provision for payment of a surviving spouse's pension. However, an often overlooked issue relates to the identification of the deceased member's spouse *on a date specified by the scheme.*

In particular it must be identified whether scheme benefits are to be paid to the member's spouse at date of retirement or to the spouse at the date of the member's death. Take the following example:

Example – Joe

Joe was a member of a generous final salary scheme which has, since his retirement eight years ago, been paying him a pension of £12,000 each year. There is provision within the scheme for a surviving spouse's pension to be paid on his death, equal to two-thirds of the pension payable to Joe (thus £8,000 each year). At the time of his retirement Joe was married to Marie but the couple divorced five years ago. Joe has subsequently married Janet, although that marriage quickly deteriorated and, though not divorced, they have for some months lived apart. Joe unfortunately died last month. Does Marie receive the spouse's pension, or does Janet?

The answer depends on whether the scheme defines spouse as the spouse at date of retirement (in which case, of course, Marie would receive the pension) or the spouse at date of death (Janet). Occupational final salary schemes are divided pretty evenly between these two definitions and you should be able to identify the circumstances in which the definition used by a particular scheme could critically affect the member's choice of whether to transfer to an alternative annuity option at, or shortly before, retirement.

For example, if the scheme defines spouse as that existing at date of retirement, yet the member is not married at date of retirement, then no spouse's pension can ever become payable even if the member subsequently marries. In these circumstances the spouse's pension is of no value. Alternatively, if that member *is* married, but his wife predeceases him then, again, no spouse's pension can ever become payable, even if the scheme member remarries, because his spouse as at date of retirement is dead.

Conversely, if the scheme defines spouse as at date of death but the member, married at date of retirement, subsequently divorces and does not remarry, once again a spouse's pension will not become payable.

Which definition of spouse is preferable? This depends on the current and likely future personal circumstances of the scheme member (although the author accepts this is by no means always easy or even possible to ascertain). However, it can be clearly seen that there are circumstances where a scheme member (or, more precisely, the member's spouse or former spouse) cannot possibly benefit from a survivor's pension. Here, the attractions of a possible transfer to an alternative annuity may be significant: if the transfer value reflects the promise of a spouse's pension (even though none can become payable) this additional value may be transferred to provide single life only benefits, or joint life benefits using a definition of spouse more appropriate to the member's circumstances.

EARLY LEAVERS FROM OCCUPATIONAL PENSION SCHEMES (*PRESERVED PENSIONERS*)

For 'early leavers' (i.e. a member leaving employment and active membership of the scheme before normal retirement age) a 'spouse at date of retirement' definition will usually translate to 'spouse at date of leaving', and similar considerations will apply as with members remaining in employment up to normal retirement age.

LEGALLY MARRIED SPOUSES – STILL LIVING TOGETHER?

A number of final salary schemes – although it occurs much less commonly in annuities bought from insurance company providers – provide for a surviving spouse's pension (whether deemed to be spouse at date of retirement or spouse at date of death) to be payable only to a spouse who is still living with, as husband and wife, the scheme member at the date of his death. Developing the example of Joe, Marie (his first wife) and Janet (second wife). As Joe and Janet were no longer living together at the date of his death (although remaining married) a scheme with what we might call this '*living together clause*' paying a pension to a surviving spouse (whether as at date of retirement or as at date of death) would make payments to neither Marie nor Janet.

You should be able to immediately identify the increased number of circumstances in which a scheme imposing the 'living together' clause will not make surviving spouse's payments where, perhaps, they were expected to be made.

The author is particularly aware of a very large public limited company whose scheme includes a 'living together' clause that staunchly refused (and is still refusing) to pay a spouse's pension to a widow who was not living with her husband – a former employee of the company – at the time of his death. In fact, the reason for the couple not living together was that he had spent his last years in very poor health as a resident in a high intensive care nursing home while the wife remained resident in the family home! There were, the scheme argues, certain aspects of the relationship which tempted the trustees not to pay the widow by using their discretionary powers (as one would expect the vast majority of trustees to do) but nonetheless this represents a very lucid and regrettable example of the potential application of the 'living together' clause.

DEFINITION OF (LEGALLY MARRIED) SPOUSE – FINANCIAL PLANNING IMPLICATIONS

It is clearly important for a financial adviser to determine the definition of spouse for members of occupational pension schemes in determining which spouse (i.e. that at retirement, or at death) would be paid a pension, and whether the 'living together' condition has been adopted. The 'spouse' unable to expect such a pension could be well advised, of course, to make alternative financial provision against the death of his or her spouse.

It is equally important for advisers of 'bought' pension annuities from insurance company providers to ensure that the definition of spouse (at death or at retirement) matches the circumstances, requirements, and perception of the parties involved. There is, in fact, relatively very little difference in rates (about 1% or less) where an insurance company offers a choice of 'at retirement' or 'at death' definitions, the latter offering slightly less favourable rates because the underwriter assumes that remarriage, if it occurs, will take place, with a younger partner!

As regards 'early leavers' from final salary pension schemes, it is usually the case that the transfer value offered by the scheme represents in part (often around 25% of the total value) the value of the promise of a spouse's pension even though the definition of spouse/dependant used by the scheme would appear to preclude any such benefit (e.g. the member is not married). In these circumstances, we would suggest, the benefits of a transfer to a private pension arrangement (under which the client can, in effect, select his preferred definition) may be heightened.

Overall, financial advisers must be mindful of checking the definition of spouse in all cases, bringing this to the attention of their clients.

COMMON-LAW SPOUSES

Beyond the apparently simple, but in practice not nearly so simple, duty of determining the existence of a spouse's pension, scheme definitions of 'dependant' vary wildly. Always (at least as far as the author is aware) a dependent child will qualify for a dependant's pension on the death of the scheme member. More controversial issues exist around dependent adults, and in particular dependent adult 'partners' (in a sexual sense), of scheme members where such a relationship exists outside of legal marriage (without putting too fine a point on it!).

One thing we know for certain is that such partners cannot qualify for inclusion in the standard definition of 'spouse' (invariably defining spouse within strict legal terms). However, it could be argued that they could or should be included as a potential recipient of survivor's pension benefits under the definition of 'dependant'.

Another thing we know for certain is that the Inland Revenue has confirmed that it is comfortable from a scheme approval point of view in *allowing* dependant pension benefits to be paid to adult dependants (although, it should be noted, only if the survivor can demonstrate that he or she was financially dependent on the deceased at the date of death).

This does not mean to say, however, that schemes *have* to pay a pension to such partners, merely that they *can if they want to*. Most schemes do not, or at least (within final salary schemes) they do not commit themselves to making such payments, preferring instead to leave payments to the discretion of the scheme trustees.

The issues involved here are numerous, not least emanating from the lack of legal definition of 'common-law spouse': just how long does a couple have to be living together before they can legitimately call themselves 'common-law husband and wife': ten years, five years, one year ... one night? There is no legal definition in the UK and so schemes – quite apart from the financial considerations of having to pay many more claimant survivors – have tended to avoid committing or even allowing the trustees to make such payments to any adult dependants other than legally married spouses.

This reluctance, though, has been challenged over the years, although usually only on an individual case-by-case basis in the light of very individual circumstances. The likely success of such a challenge, if made in the courts, has taken a blow following the European ruling on the case of *Lisa Grant v. South West Trains* (the details of which are outlined below) which, although relating to *same sex* partners, may have some influence over the claim of common-law 'spouses' in its failed attempt to bind trustees to make dependant pension payments to someone other than legally married spouses.

Before discussing the Lisa Grant case in more detail, and its implications, it is worth noting the difference in Scotland. Here, it is possible for an unmarried couple (or, indeed, either one of the couple), living together in circumstances which the rest of the UK would describe as a common-law relationship, to apply to the court to have their relationship deemed as 'married by habit and repute' meaning, broadly, by length of relationship and the way that relationship has been perceived by their acquaintances. This application can be made even after the death of one of the partners and frequently occurs where one of the partners seeks certainty of receipt of spouse's benefits from a pension scheme.

In any event, once again the financial planning implications are clear: if a client is in a 'common-law partner' relationship the provisions and practice of the client's pension scheme should be investigated to ascertain the most appropriate recommendation. A number of the country's leading pension annuity offices will effect a 'joint life' (anomaly: see earlier text) pension for an annuity with a common-law spouse although, technically at least, financial dependency on the scheme member must be provable by the 'second life'.

Finally it is worth noting that a number of life insurance companies offer 'joint life' pension annuities with a named common-law partner. However, it should also be noted that the requirement is for that annuity provider to confirm the claimant was financially dependant on the deceased at the date of death. Although the author is aware that certain insurance companies may not require too much evidence of dependency, nonetheless the possibility must be recognized that the annuitant may during his lifetime be accepting a much lower annuity payment as a result of purchasing a dependant's pension which may never become payable.

SAME-SEX PARTNERS

As we have just discussed, many schemes are prepared to consider the merits, on a case-by-case basis, of a claim by a common-law spouse to dependant's pension benefits, although a significant number stipulate they will only pay an adult claimant who is legally married to the deceased scheme member.

Far fewer schemes, though, are prepared to consider paying a same-sex partner of a deceased pension scheme member. Most refuse altogether to recognize homosexual adults as beneficiaries, although the number of these 'refusniks' is falling quite rapidly.

The Inland Revenue has confirmed a number of years ago that schemes *may* pay a dependant's pension benefit to a same-sex partner but, as with common-law partners, a homosexual claimant must be able to show financial dependency on the deceased at date of death. Furthermore, as with common-law partners' claims, schemes may refuse to consider them altogether or may elect to consider each claim on its merits. Note that schemes cannot *promise* to pay all such claimants due not least to the *financial dependency* requirement and the absence of any definition of *same-sex partner* (as regards the period of time they must have cohabited to qualify as such).

The rights of same-sex partners in pension scheme benefits were clarified by the very important law case in which a lady by the name of Lisa Grant took her employers, South West Trains, to court claiming that they sexually discriminated against her (in contravention of Article 119 of the Treaty of Rome).

LISA GRANT V. SOUTH WEST TRAINS

Lisa Grant was an employee of South West Trains and had a lesbian partner who was refused the benefit of concessionary rail travel with that employer, leading to a claim for sex discrimination.

South West Trains granted concessionary rail travel to married couples and, indeed, to common-law spouses (i.e. partners of the opposite sex living together, but not legally married). They did not, however, grant such a benefit to lesbian partners and so the claim for sex discrimination was brought before an English tribunal. The tribunal decided this was a case of sex discrimination and therefore found against South West Trains.

It was understandable that relatively little interest was stirred by this case, probably due to the seemingly small proportion of the population who would be affected by rights to concessionary rail travel. However, the case was most notably important, not for the rights to concessionary rail travel, but for the right to pension scheme benefits.

Large occupational pension schemes such as that operated by South West Trains almost invariably grant a pension to the surviving spouse of a deceased scheme member.

Historically, such a benefit has been offered only to legally married partners though, more recently, an increasing number of schemes have – usually at the discretion of the trustees – granted such a pension to surviving partners of the opposite sex, although only (at least in theory) where that partner can show some elements of financial dependency on the deceased.

Far fewer schemes, although still an increasing number, may also pay a surviving partner's pension to a surviving homosexual partner of the deceased who must be able to demonstrate financial dependency on the former scheme member.

It is important to note, however, that schemes are not *obliged* to include a surviving spouse's pension as part of the scheme benefits although, as noted above, this is almost invariably a major part of scheme design. More importantly, even where schemes offer a surviving spouse's pension, they are not obliged to extend that benefit to partners not legally married to deceased scheme members.

Even where such partners *may* benefit from such a pension this will invariably depend on the partner being able to prove financial dependency on the deceased and, even then, payment will almost invariably be at the trustees' discretion on a case-by-case basis. If Lisa Grant could show that South West Trains ought not to discriminate against same-sex partners and must therefore, as the English tribunal decided, pay concessionary rail travel to such partners where this benefit is offered to legally-married spouses, then it would be a very short step to forcing employers to offer a surviving partner's pension where such a pension was offered to legally-married partners.

Thus the interest in the Lisa Grant case extended far beyond the realms of concessionary rail travel. The implications for pension schemes were (and are) huge: the cost of providing surviving partners' pensions to homosexual partners, and perhaps more pertinently and expensively to opposite-sex partners who are not legally married to scheme members, would be extremely expensive.

Not least, pension schemes were concerned that if they were forced to offer this benefit to an extended range of potential beneficiaries the question would regularly arise as to whether a claimant was indeed a partner of the deceased scheme member to the extent required to qualify them for benefits under the pension scheme. For example, just how long should the two people (the deceased and the claimant) have been living together to appropriately call the survivor a partner? There is no legal definition of a *common-law spouse* and therefore no defined period of time of cohabitation for which such a phrase could be justified. The potential problems for pension schemes were huge.

Accordingly the case was referred to the European Court of Justice, which considered the claim for sex discrimination under Article 119 of the Treaty of Rome. This Court overturned the decision by the English tribunal and found in favour of South West Trains. Pension schemes breathed a huge sigh of relief.

But why did the European court overturn the English tribunal's decision? They explained, quite simply, that Article 119 of the Treaty of Rome related to discrimination between males and females. South West Trains did indeed exclude from benefits homosexual female partners but they also excluded homosexual *male* partners and so did not discriminate between males and females, treating both male and female homosexual relationships exactly the same (i.e. excluding them from benefits). The discrimination by South West Trains was therefore not between males and females but between heterosexuals and homosexuals.

SEXUALITY DISCRIMINATION IN PENSION SCHEMES: LISA GRANT AND BEYOND

The term *sexuality discrimination* has since been coined to describe this discrimination which does not contravene either Article 119 of the Treaty of Rome, nor any other articles or legislation within the European Community – or for that matter any legislation in the UK. Thus Lisa Grant's claim for sex discrimination could not, and ultimately did not, succeed. That remains the situation.

The fact that Lisa Grant lost the case served to further confirm the ability of schemes to select a definition of dependant without being legally bound to recognize common-law spouses or same-sex partners. It is, as the Lisa Grant case has confirmed, perfectly acceptable in law to discriminate between homosexuals and heterosexuals in the provision of any benefits by an employer – in particular, for the purposes of this book, pension scheme benefits.

However, following pressure from public interest groups the Government commissioned a report to look into the advisability (or otherwise) of introducing legislation to force pension schemes to recognize same-sex partners for surviving dependant's pension benefits. At time of writing this report had just been submitted to the Government, recommending that pension schemes *should* be made to consider paying (or, indeed, forced to pay) same-sex partners such a pension. This would clearly have a knock-on effect to common-law partners also, and the costs to pension schemes, as outlined above, would be huge. We await the Government's response (still not given, now three months after publication of the recommendation).

DEFINITION OF SPOUSE AND DEPENDANT: SUMMARY

In considering various annuity or retirement income options the retiree should seek to ensure as a matter of great importance that the preferred option will, or at the very least probably will (for example, due to proof of financial dependence) pay death benefits (including a survivor's pension) to the individual(s) preferred by the individual scheme member – obviously, according to his or her personal circumstances. Retirees should be aware that the value of a survivor's pension can quite easily exceed 25% of the total value of retirement benefits, and so the loss or omission of such a benefit would indicate a very costly reduction in value.

6 With Profit and Unit-Linked Annuities

INTRODUCTION

The basic concept behind an annuity purchase is traditionally that a person obtains a guaranteed income in return for the capital retained by the annuity provider. The rate of return provided in relation to the capital bears a direct relationship to the underlying rate of investment return that the insurance company can obtain upon primarily, long-dated gilts.

Until the mid-1990s most annuitants were relatively happy with this state of affairs (not least perhaps because there was no real alternative). The only real risk to the annuitant, apart from dying too early and therefore not having obtained a worthwhile benefit from the capital kept by the annuity provider, was that inflation would progressively reduce the purchasing power of the annuity. However, even with returns being guaranteed, an annuitant could have a lower starting annuity with either a provision of set rates of increase each year (for example 3% or 5% per annum) or, with some providers, rates of increase linked to increases in the Retail Price Index. The annuity providers protect themselves by buying appropriate index-linked gilts.

The 1990s have seen a huge growth in the introduction of various alternatives to these conventional annuities.

CHANGES IN THE 1990S

Falling gilt rates

During the 1990s gilt rates fell substantially to historic lows to a point where the rate of annuity being offered, especially to people in their 60s or younger, was sometimes lower than the rate of return that could be obtained from cash deposits (or certainly not much higher). By illustration, in 1990, a male aged 65 could obtain an annuity rate of 15.5% per annum but in 1999 the same man could only obtain an annuity rate of 9.5 % per annum. Although in the 1990s inflation was relatively low, many retiring people clearly were reluctant to lock their capital into low rates of interest for the rest of their lives, bearing in mind that life expectancy is now such that many people can expect to be retired for at least half the number of years for which they were at work.

In addition to the prospect that increases in inflation would make inroads into the purchasing power of any annuity obtained (as with any annuity in the past), the additional problem of progressively lower annuity rates and increased life expectancy developed

New options
Unfortunately for those people retiring, with pension funds to vest, low interest and annuity rates created an unavoidable problem that they were forced to buy an annuity based on underlying interest rates. They had no way of securing their future retirement income on 'real assets' such as equities or property – both of which provided much higher rates of return than those available on conventional annuities.

Due to these factors, annuity providers started to market annuities where future income could be linked more to asset-backed investments rather than gilt returns. Under these alternatives, with profits or unit-linked annuities, the level of annuity income is related to the future performance of the underlying investment fund.

With longer life expectancy combined with the belief that in the longer term equities may be expected to outperform fixed-interest investments, there may be much to said for having future income linked to equity-based investments. If capital is coming from a pension scheme, the bulk of the capital growth within the pension scheme fund will have come from investments in equities so, the reasoning goes, it makes sense to have income in retirement similarly linked to the equity market. This is particularly relevant for a person retiring relatively young. It is also a very useful option for those who have other sources of income or, alternatively, can form part of an overall annuity purchase plan.

Either type of annuity, whether with profits or unit-linked, will generally have an initial annuity payment lower than the equivalent level conventional annuity. However, when conventional annuities have a low starting level, when (as now) market interest rates are low, the difference between the two starting levels becomes less pronounced.

TYPES OF PENSION ARRANGEMENT FOR WHICH UNIT LINKING AND WITH PROFITS ANNUITIES ARE AN OPTION

When first available, these alternatives were available only for those arrangements where the annuity was being purchased from 'free' capital in the hands of the investor (i.e. for a purchased life annuity). However, they are now available for annuity purchases from occupational pension schemes, free-standing additional voluntary contributions (FSAVCs), personal pensions and retirement annuities.

A pension fund arising from having been contracted out of SERPS cannot be used to purchase these types of annuity because of the guarantees that have to be applied to any annuity purchased from the protected rights part of the fund.

Occupational pensions – maximum benefits

If the annuity is being provided from a fund arising from an occupational pension scheme or FSAVC, the increases in annuity rate will be limited to those allowable under the Inland Revenue limits, although should this rule have a restricting impact in any particular year, the unused potential increase would not be lost; it would be held back until a later year when it may be able to be added.

Example:

Let us assume that the maximum allowable annuity from an occupational pension scheme is £10,000 per year. We know, from Chapter 3, this limits increases in payment, in line with increases in the Retail Price Index, as the following table illustrates.

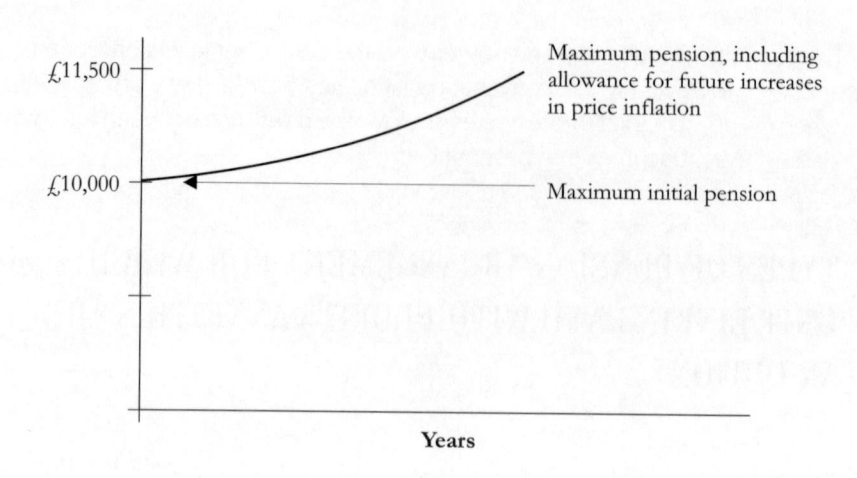

[Graph: showing £11,500 "Maximum pension, including allowance for future increases in price inflation" curving upward from £10,000 "Maximum initial pension", plotted against Years]

Let us also assume that the starting pension from an annuity is, say, £8,000 and as a result of escalation rises to £12,000 in three years' time, by which time inflation has risen by 15%. The Inland Revenue maximum becomes £11,500 (£10,000 plus 15%) and so the full value of the investment growth cannot be taken.

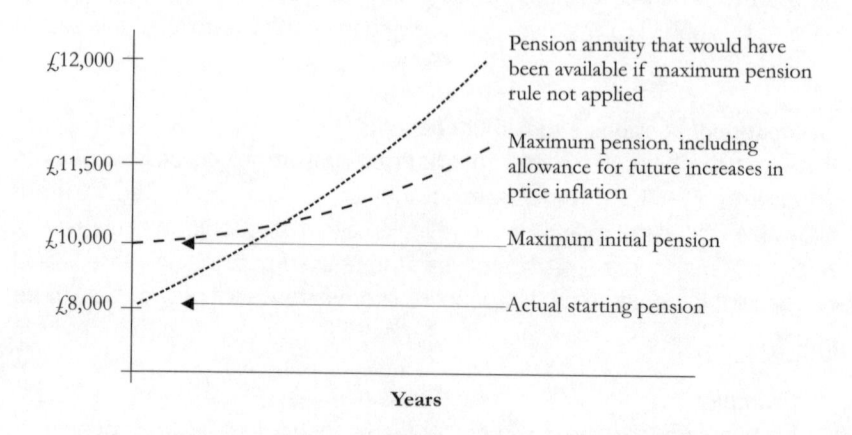

[Graph: showing £12,000 "Pension annuity that would have been available if maximum pension rule not applied", £11,500 "Maximum pension, including allowance for future increases in price inflation", £10,000 "Maximum initial pension", and £8,000 "Actual starting pension", plotted against Years]

If, though, we take a lower starting point and a reasonable assumed rate of growth, the situation could well become:

WITH PROFIT AND UNIT-LINKED ANNUITIES

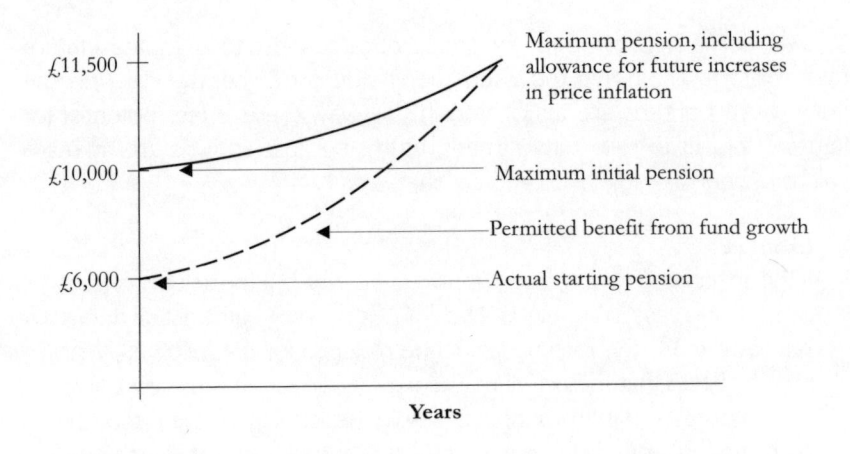

£11,500 — Maximum pension, including allowance for future increases in price inflation

£10,000 — Maximum initial pension

— Permitted benefit from fund growth

£6,000 — Actual starting pension

Years

WITH PROFIT ANNUITIES

The purchase monies of the annuity is invested into the with profits fund of the insurance company, and the income is derived from a guaranteed level of payments which provides a basic income. In addition, investment earnings, passed on by way of bonuses, increase that basic income.

Broadly speaking, with profits annuities fall into three main categories:

- Conventional with profits
- With profits plus guarantees
- Unitized with profits

Conventional with profits

With the conventional with profits annuity the insurance company declares a starting income which, as the company declares future reversionary bonuses, is increased to reflect the bonuses added. There may also be provision for a terminal bonus. Unlike a typical with profits policy, payment of a terminal bonus on maturity or earlier death is not appropriate with an annuity, so each year a calculation of a notional terminal bonus over and above any annual reversionary bonus is made. This can either be consolidated with the annual bonus to arrive at a total bonus or given separately.

With some arrangements, the annuitant can choose to anticipate a future rate of return. The higher the assumption made, the higher the initial income but, where bonuses are anticipated in this way, there is less potential for future increases to reflect investment returns because some of the increase will have been already taken into account.

Example:
If the anticipated reversionary bonus rate is 4%, but the actual bonus is 5%, the increase in annuity will be 1%. Conversely, if the actual bonus rate is only 3% the income would be reduced for the following year by 1%. Note that the actual mathematical calculation is usually a little more complex than this simple example, depending on the insurance company provider, but the end result is very close to that illustrated.

When gilt rates are high the bonus rate that has to be assumed to match a conventional level annuity is also high but, conversely, when gilt rates are low the bonus rate that has to be anticipated for a with profits annuity to enable the starting income to be the same as for a conventional level annuity is also low.

With profits plus guarantees

The with profits annuity with guarantees works in a similar way to the conventional with profits annuity but, here, the insurance company provides an annuity guarantee that the annuity will never fall below the initial starting income. Obviously, this guarantee comes at a cost in that the level of starting income is less than would be the case without such a guarantee. Here it is important to ascertain the company's practice as regards the declaration of the reversionary bonus and terminal bonus.

Unitized with profits

Unitized with profits annuities are arrangements where the annuitant secures a number of units in the with profits fund of an insurance company in the same way as any other unit-linked fund can be purchased (see unit-linked funds below).

Unlike other asset-linked unitized funds, with profits funds enable the annuitant to obtain the benefit of a smoothing out of investment returns and therefore less potential volatility to the income payable. Regular bonuses are declared and these increase the unit price. Once added, they cannot be removed. If the returns being achieved are higher than anticipated, the company may decide that it will add a supplementary bonus in the same way as a terminal bonus addition which can, though, be reduced or removed at any time.

THE IMPORTANCE OF THE 'ASSUMED BONUS RATE', AND OTHER ASSUMPTIONS, IN WITH PROFITS ANNUITIES

If the annuitant selects a very low level of assumed reversionary bonus the starting level of the pension will be low. However, as you should be able to identify from the simple example above, such a low assumption would give substantial potential for future growth in the income generated from the annuity. As an extreme example, if the annuitant assumes 'nil' future bonuses, then any bonuses declared in future years would increase the annuity payable from then on: a 5% reversionary bonus would increase the annuity payment by (broadly) 5% (plus any terminal bonus), and so on.

However, a high assumed bonus level could leave the annuitant open to a fall in future income levels. Continuing our example, if a 6% future bonus rate had been assumed yet only a 5% reversionary bonus rate declared then, in the absence of a terminal bonus payment in that year, the annuitant would suffer a 1% fall in income level.

Furthermore, it is important to note that with profits annuities are bought at outset on specific terms, and the normal range of annuity options has to be determined at outset, including whether to elect for a single life or a joint life pension, whether to select a guarantee period, and so on. The addition of such options reduces the annuity rate payable, just as with conventional annuities.

This is an important point to note: it is tempting to consider with profit annuities as an identifiable fund (which it is) which will always, at some stage, become payable to the annuitant or beneficiaries (which it won't). The with profit annuity fund 'dies' (as far as the annuitant is concerned) when he or she dies and does not become payable to beneficiaries, as is usually the case with drawdown arrangements (which we discuss in Chapters 8 and 9).

Finally you should be aware that with profits annuities cannot be used where legislation or regulations require the annuity to include certain guarantees. As an example, protected rights funds require the pension in payment to escalate to the rate of price inflation up to 3% – a guarantee that clearly cannot be given by with profits annuities. Similar considerations apply to any pension in respect of the guaranteed minimum pension under SERPS benefits. As regards occupational pension schemes, any benefits accrued after 5 April 1997 are now required to provide escalation in payment of the rate of price inflation up to 5% – again, a promise that cannot be met or given by with profits annuities. Where an individual's retirement income consists partly of these guaranteed benefits and partly of excess (non-guaranteed benefits), this guaranteed part, at the very least, must be satisfied by the purchase of a conventional guaranteed annuity.

UNIT-LINKED ANNUITIES

The purchase price is invested into a one or more of the insurance company's unit-linked funds. They operate in a similar way to with profits annuities in terms of being able to benefit over the longer term from asset-linked investments rather than being locked into the returns available from long-dated gilts, but a higher degree of risk is associated with them.

They differ from conventional with profits annuities and annuities with guarantees in the following ways.

- The income is calculated as the value of the number of units
- There is no guaranteed amount of income, but see below.

Whenever payment is due to be made the bid value of the underlying units are calculated and these form the basis of the income payable. If unit values rise, income rises and conversely, if unit prices fall then income falls: it is as simple and volatile as that!

With unit-linked annuities, as for with profit annuities, there may be provision for the annuitant to select an anticipated growth rate which therefore effects the level of the initial starting income: the higher the growth rate selected, the higher the starting income but then the increases on that income will be lower than if the initial income had been at a lower level.

If a rate of growth has been assumed and the rate of growth achieved has been greater than the assumed rate, the income will be increased, but if lower, then the income will be reduced.

PROVISION FOR A GUARANTEE ON INCOME

Generally speaking, with a unit-linked annuity, there is no provision for guarantees. However, some insurance companies operate a unit-linked type of fund which, although linked to equity prices, includes certain other investments designed to protect the fund against falling markets and, as a result, can provide for guarantees to lock in growth being achieved. Linking such a fund to an annuity arrangement enables the company to guarantee a minimum level of pension for life, but with the prospect of increases directly linked to underlying equity returns.

ADDITIONAL MATTERS RELATING TO UNIT-LINKED ANNUITIES

As we noted for with profits annuities, the annuitant has to decide at outset whether to include provision for such options as surviving spouse's pension, guarantee period, etc.

Furthermore, as for with profits annuities, although a fund value can be identified at any point in time this only (though importantly) serves to dictate the level of pension payable to the annuitant on an ongoing basis – it does not become payable on the death of the annuitant.

Finally, again as for with profits annuities, unit-linked annuities may not be used where guaranteed benefits are required – most importantly GMPs, protected rights, and wherever escalation to pensions in payment is mandatory.

WITH PROFITS AND UNIT-LINKED ANNUITIES – A SUMMARY

It would be fair and accurate to identify with profits annuities as being less volatile than unit-linked annuities, although clearly more volatile than conventional (guaranteed) annuities. With both of these options it is the investor who stands the investment risk, not the insurance company provider (as is the case with conventional annuities). This may (and does, in the opinion and experience of the author) appeal to a significant number of retirees, and to insurance company providers who can more accurately assess their future profitability in much the same way as they assess the profitability of single-premium unit-linked and with profits investments generally.

There is no doubt these annuities will grow in popularity, with steady stream of new providers entering the market. They allow annuitants to fix their future retirement income to asset-backed (largely equity-backed) returns rather than gilt and fixed-interest returns which, over the longer period at least, may be expected to underperform more volatile assets.

7 Staggered Pensions Vesting

INTRODUCTION

Although pension arrangements are thought of as being planned to provide benefits at a single certain age, it is very common to find that for various reasons a person's financial needs may be such that he or she does not require the total benefits from a pension arrangement at a particular time, but *does* need part of these benefits progressively over a period of time.

If a person has a number of different pension arrangements or policies he or she can choose to take benefits from one or more, at one time, and benefits from others later. It may be, for example, that over a number of years a person has arranged personal pensions with different companies, or even with the same company but with new policies each time. As a result he or she could have a certain degree of flexibility to take benefits at different times. However, the amount of flexibility would in these circumstances usually be very limited in that the total number of policies held would generally be just a few. Over the last decade or so the concept of issuing policies in segments has been developed, so that even with just one *policy* a person could choose to take benefits from some of the *segments* within the policy one year, from further segments another year, and so on until all the segments had been used.

This has led to the development of what is known as *phased retirement* or *staggered vesting* strategies, with pension policies being specifically designed to facilitate this. Generally, policies issued with this requirement in mind would have, say, 1,000 separate clusters, or segments, within a single policy.

Although personal pension polices have been specifically mentioned, a person in an occupational pension scheme, or a person who has retirement annuity policies, may arrange to have a transfer made to a personal pension arrangement to achieve the ability to phase the taking of benefits. Note that it is not possible to phase benefits from an occupational pension scheme.

With a transfer from an occupational scheme, Inland Revenue restrictions in respect of tax-free cash that applied under the occupational scheme would still be applied. Further restrictions may apply on death benefits, as noted in Chapter 2.

THE CONCEPT OF STAGGERED VESTING

By having a number of different personal pension policies or segments within a single policy, an individual can have increased flexibility by taking benefits from different arrangements at different times between the ages of 50 and 75, and thus 'phasing retirement'.

The concept of vesting different policies or segments at different ages has for *many* years been used by individuals who do not entirely retire on one date, but phase in their retirement. Hence the commonly used descriptive title 'phased retirement'.

For the specific purposes of the concepts in this chapter the author believes the title 'staggered vesting' to be generally more technically accurate because this describes the situation where the vesting of different pension policies is staggered over a number of years, notwithstanding the possibility that the individual might completely retire on one single date.

Each year an individual's income needs may be assessed, noting the level of income available from existing sources, and calculating the shortfall of income to expenditure. To meet this shortfall a sufficient number of pension policy segments are vested such that the tax-free cash plus the residual pension (after tax) are sufficient to 'bridge the gap'.

The remaining segments remain within the (tax-sheltered) pension fund to grow. Given reasonable investment returns achieved by the remaining fund and/or rising annuity rates as a consequence of getting older, it may be possible to achieve a steadily rising income. There is, however, the very real risk that investment performance may fall well short of expectations and/or that annuity rates may fall if interest rates fall, in which case the staggered vesting strategy may result in potentially severe financial loss.

Because the individual's required annual income is met by the *entire proceeds* of the vested pension segments, the availability of the tax-free cash sum of itself at retirement is lost, making this type of approach unsuitable for those who had specific plans for the tax-free cash sum itself. This may arise, for example, if the personal pension member has an interest-only mortgage and planned to repay the advance from the tax-free cash sum.

At age 75, under current legislation, any cluster policies remaining have to be vested and pension benefits taken.

SOME REASONS FOR STAGGERED VESTING

There can be many reasons for a person deciding that it is to his or her advantage to stagger the taking of benefits from pension arrangements. The examples given below are not necessarily exhaustive, but are to illustrate some of the reasons potentially appropriate to individuals in certain circumstances.

Annuity rates based on a relatively young age

The retiring person may decide that the annuity rates being offered based on age are unattractive and is loathe to commit the total pension fund to the purchase of an annuity at the time. This is of particular relevance for younger ages. As an alternative only the minimum amount of fund needed to produce the total required income in a year will be used, with the remaining fund left until such time as, with increasing age, annuity rates become more attractive.

Reducing income but not fully retiring

It may be that a person is retiring from employment but carrying on with a self-employed source of income, or developing an existing source of income more fully. He or she may therefore not need the full benefits from the occupational pension scheme but cannot cope financially without encashing part of the pension rights accrued.

Similarly a self-employed person may wish to reduce working hours but still continue earning and does not need all the income that the existing pension arrangements could provide at one time. Particular examples include solicitors and accountants who may cease full time commitments but continue to work in a consultancy capacity for increasingly fewer regular hours as the years progress.

Retiring before state pension age
A person may have accrued entitlement to a worthwhile state pension but, as he or she is retiring before state pension age, may wish to plan on the basis that the needs for annuity income will be less once the state pension becomes payable. Although earlier vested policies will still be providing ongoing income, because much of the year-by-year 'income' as a policy is vested has been provided up to state pension age from the tax-free cash sum, he or she can choose at that time not to vest any further policies until such time as additional income is again required.

A pension scheme member has remaining short-term commitments
It may be the case that when a person is retiring, either completely or partly, he or she has certain commitments remaining for a limited period. He or she may therefore wish to ensure that there is income to meet those commitments but knows that, all things being equal, the need for income will reduce. Consequently, he or she may not wish to take all the pension benefits upon retirement – restricting vesting parts of the fund to only what is needed on a year-by-year basis.

A pension scheme member is in poor health
The taking of an annuity from a pension arrangement involves loss of capital to dependants. If a pension scheme member is in poor health he or she may prefer to arrange matters so that, in the event of early death, as much of the fund as possible is left for dependants. The concept of a guarantee period, or even a 50% spouse's pension, may not be attractive when compared to the survivors being able to have full benefit of the remaining pension fund – usually free of liability to tax.

A pension scheme member is not married but has a partner
If a member is not married at retirement but wishes to protect the interests of a common-law or same-sex partner, there may be an advantage to be gained in taking the maximum single life annuity required to meet needs on a year-by-year basis, leaving the remaining fund written in trust for the partner. Upon death of the member (provided that it occurs before age 75) the surviving partner will receive a capital sum that can be used, say, to provide an ongoing income.

STAGGERED VESTING PLANNING IN PRACTICE

The example on page 110 overleaf is based upon a male life reaching the age of 60 and illustrates the way in which taking benefits on a staggered vesting basis could be more beneficial than taking all the benefits at retirement age. In reading through this example, the reader should bear in mind that the annuity rates vary from time to time and investment returns will almost certainly differ from the average (9%) assumption. Therefore we stress that it is more important to consider the *implications* of the results rather than dwell upon the illustrated figures themselves.

Retirement Income Planning

Age	Value Fund	Amount of Pension Fund Vested	Tax-Free Cash Obtained in Year	Net Pension after Basic Rate Tax	Total Net Income Produced from Vested Segments in Year	Total Net Annuity Income when Annuities from Previous Vestings Added	Total Net Income in Year Provided by Annuity plus Tax-free Cash in Year	Remaining Fund
	£	£	£	£	£	£	£	£
60	200,000	40,437	10,109	1,877	11,986	1,877	11,986	159,000
61	162,000	33,561	8,390	1,731	10,121	3,608	11,998	128,000
62	138,000	27,755	6,939	1,451	8,390	5,059	11,998	111,000
63	120,000	22,896	5,724	1,251	6,975	6,274	11,998	97,200
64	105,000	18,837	4,709	1,015	5,724	7,288	11,998	86,200
65	93,100	15,455	3,864	846	4,710	8,134	11,998	77,700
66	83,900	12,642	3,161	703	3,864	8,837	11,998	71,300
67	77,000	10,309	2,577	583	3,160	9,421	11,998	66,700
68	72,100	8,379	2,095	483	2,578	9,903	11,998	63,700
69	68,800	6,787	1,697	398	2,095	10,301	11,998	62,100
70	67,100	5,477	1,369	327	1,696	10,629	11,998	61,600
71	66,500	4,403	1,101	268	1,369	10,897	11,998	62,100
72	68,700	3,526	831	219	1,050	11,116	11,998	63,600
73	68,700	2,811	703	179	882	11,295	11,998	65,900
74	71,200	2,232	558	145	703	11,440	11,998	69,000
75	74,600	74,600	18,653	4,951	23,604	16,391	35,044	NIL

Note
- It is assumed that the fund grows at 9% per annum. The apparent lower rate of growth in the first year illustrates the effects of the initial charges.
- A quotation from an annuity life office at this time shows that if, at age 60, the placeholder had taken his total benefits and applied them to purchase an annuity including a 50% spouse's benefit, based upon the

rate applicable at age 60 his net annuity would have been £11,998 per annum.
- The annuity illustrated is based upon a single life annuity (for reasons given later in this chapter).

EXPLANATION OF THE ILLUSTRATION

At age 60 (reading across the line)

With an initial fund value of £200,000 (column 2) and a target net annual income of £11,998 – to match the net income available from immediate vesting of all the fund – the computer calculates the need to vest £40,437 of the fund (column 3). Of this £40,437 we know that 25% may be taken as a tax-free lump sum – £10,109 (column 4). This leaves £30,328 of the vested fund which must be used to purchase an annuity which, at the rates assumed in the illustration, would yield a net pension after basic-rate tax of £1,877 (column 5). Adding the tax-free cash (£10,109) and the residual net pension (£1,877) gives a total net annual income in this first year of £11,986 (column 6) – as near as matters exactly the annual target income.

Column 7 is not really relevant in this first year, simply re-iterating the net annuity provided so far, and column 8 does no more than confirm that the net income provided for that year matches the target originally established, being the net income from a conventional annuity.

Column 9 illustrates that, after vesting £40,437 of the fund, £159,000 (allowing for some rounding of figures) remains.

Second year of the staggered vesting strategy

If we now look at the second year of the staggered vesting strategy (annuitant now aged 61), column 2 illustrates the expectation that the fund at the start of the year will be £162,000, this being the £159,000 remaining from year one, plus growth (in this illustration assumed to be 9%), less charges imposed by the insurance company product provider. It should be noted, with this particular example, that in the first year of the strategy charges eat into almost all of the fund growth. This is not uncommon among insurance companies with products of this nature.

Column 3, in this second year, is a figure calculated by the computer program as being the amount of fund that must be vested in this year to maintain the overall net income required (in this case, at a little under £12,000). The vesting of £33,561 (column 3) produces tax-free cash of £8,390 (column 4, being ¼ of the figure in column 3, obviously) and a residual annuity of £1,731 (column 5). The total net income produced from the vested segments in Year 2 is therefore £10,121 (column 6, being the totals from columns 4 and 5). Column 7 shows the annual income produced from the vested segments in both Years 1 and 2 (£1,877 from year one + £1,731 from year two = £3,608 per annum in total). The relevance of this 'running total' will be better understood when we have explained Year 2's column 8.

Now, we know that our target income for Year 2 is assumed to be £11,998 and, in Year 2 of the strategy, this is made up of three component parts:
i) tax-free cash from the part of the fund vested in Year 2, plus
ii) the residual annuity from the remainder of the fund vested in Year 2 (which could not be taken as tax-free cash), plus
iii) the annuity income purchased in Year 1 (£1,877, from column 7 in Year 1) which, of course, continues until the annuitant's death.

Finally, column 9 shows the fund remaining after Year 2's vesting of £33,561 is deducted from the starting fund of £162,000.

Third year of the staggered vesting strategy

Don't worry: we are not going to explain every line of the illustration; there is no need to! It is, though, we feel, useful to look at the third year of the illustration, and the very last year, because certain differences over the first two years become apparent.

Column 2 (for age 62) shows the starting assumed fund of £138,000 being the fund remaining from Year 2 (£128,000) plus growth (9%) less charges, and with an allowance for rounding. Remember that the fund growth of 9% does not apply only on the final fund remaining at the end of Year 2 of £128,000 – the fund has been steadily depleted on a monthly basis during that year from a starting figure of £162,000, thereby generating more growth than simply 9% of £128,000.

Column 3 notes that the computer program has calculated that, if everything has happened exactly according to plan in the first two years of the strategy and if the annuitant wants to maintain the same level of income, a further £27,755 of the fund must be vested in this year: £6,939 of which would be tax-free cash (column 4) with the remainder being used to buy an annuity of £1,451 (column 5). Adding together the tax-free cash and the residual annuity from the fund vested in this third year gives a net income of £8,390 (column 6).

Now, when this net income from Year 3 is added to the continuing annuities bought in Years 1 and 2 (£3,608, from column 7 in the last year) the total net income produced from this strategy in the third year of operation is, again, £11,998 – as shown in column 8. Column 8 shows the total level of ongoing conventional annuity 'bought' up to this time.

I recommend that you follow these principles through the years following Year 3 (noting that different providers of these schemes illustrate the year-by-year progression in different ways), but special mention should now be made of the illustration relating to the final year of the strategy.

Final year

As noted in Chapter 2, personal pension funds must be vested no later than the member's age 75 and so all existing segments remaining in the personal pension policy at that age must be used to buy a conventional annuity.

In our illustration the remaining fund is valued at £74,600 (column 2). All of this, vesting in this final year of the strategy (column 3), would provide a tax-free lump sum of £18,653 (column 4) with a residual net annuity of £4,951 (column 5). For this last vested segment the total net income in that year would be £23,604 (column 6) which, when added to the conventional annuities purchased in previous years (£11,440, from last year's column 7) provides a net income in that year of £35,044 (column 8) with an ongoing annuity for life, after this year, of £16,391 (column 7) – comfortably in excess of the level of income targeted at outset.

COMMENTS ON THE STANDARD ILLUSTRATION

We have spent some considerable time, in the last section, on analysing a standard illustration for a staggered vesting retirement strategy. However, it would be most unusual if circumstances or the client's personal requirements

were to proceed for the next fifteen years or so as might have been assumed at outset. Within this staggered vesting strategy there are a great many variables – both from the start of the strategy and during its lifetime – which, combined, help to illustrate the potential risks and rewards of following this retirement income option. The most important of these include (as we discuss in more depth, below):
- availability of tax-free cash
- target income to be used
- flexibility of income, up to age 75
- accumulating net income from annuities previously 'bought'
- choice of annuity basis for each year's vested segments
- direction of death benefits
- buying a spouse's pension at age 75
- future estimates of annuity rates
- investment return

AVAILABILITY OF TAX-FREE CASH

It can clearly be seen from this illustration that the tax-free cash available from the vested personal pension fund is being used, in effect, to 'subsidize' the required net annual income; it cannot be considered as being available for 'free' spending outside of this purpose. If, therefore, a retiree wants or needs some, most or (especially) all of the tax-free cash for some other purpose than this ongoing subsidy of annual outgoings, the staggered vesting strategy cannot be considered.

Moreover, particular care should be taken where the staggered vesting strategy is being considered for monies transferred from an occupational pension scheme. Here, the tax-free cash will be limited (on the assumption that we are looking at people who are at, or close to, retirement, age) to the lower of:
 a) the tax-free cash payable under the occupational pension; and
 b) the tax-free cash payable under the personal pension (25% of the fund).

If the tax-free cash from the occupational pension scheme is significantly higher than 25% of the fund (which it could easily be, depending on the final remuneration of the retiree), the reduction in availability of tax-free cash – both subjectively and taking into account taxation considerations if used to buy an annuity (see Chapter 4) – may outweigh any benefits available from the staggered vesting strategy.

Example
Mr Jones is a member of an occupational pension scheme with a fund of £100,000 and tax-free cash calculated as £60,000. He does not need the lump sum but sees the merit in – at the very least – taking it anyhow and re-investing it into a purchased life annuity (he gains exemption from tax on the capital content arising from the £60,000 PLA purchase).
If he were to transfer to a personal pension his maximum tax-free cash would fall to only £25,000 (25% of the fund). It is possible to calculate an actual financial loss, being tax exemption on the capital content of £35,000 worth of the PLA (the fall in tax-free cash).

In this respect the author feels strongly that the target net annuity figure should not assume that, if staggered vesting were not followed, the retiree would use all of his fund to buy an annuity – he would take the maximum amount of tax-free cash and re-invest it (if the intention was to provide the highest possible level of retirement income) in a purchased life annuity, thereby enjoying a tax advantage on the capital element of the new annuity. This issue has, I am afraid, been lost on most product providers who continue to assume in their illustrations that the client might have elected not to take the maximum amount of tax-free cash.

If, on the other hand, the tax-free cash available from the occupational scheme is significantly lower than 25% of the fund, the staggered vesting cannot work at all: the tax-free cash subsidizes the annuity income to provide the retiree's desired net spendable income and so, if that tax-free cash availability falls far short of 25%, the annuitant would have to vest too great a proportion of his fund, too early into the strategy, to make staggered vesting feasible in the longer term.

Example
Mrs Jones is reaching retirement age with a fund in an occupational pension scheme of £100,000 and tax-free cash at £15,000. If she transfers to a personal pension (essential if the staggered vesting strategy is to be followed) her tax-free cash is only 15% of the fund and (without going into the exact mathematics) would require far too great a proportion of her fund to be vested in the first two or three years of the staggered vesting strategy to make it viable.

The desire for, and the availability of, tax-free cash from the pension contract must be closely borne in mind when considering the potential effectiveness of the staggered vesting strategy for retirees – especially those within occupational pension schemes.

WHAT 'TARGET INCOME' SHOULD BE USED?

The higher the assumed level of conventional annuity income, the higher the amount of fund which will have to be vested from the staggered vesting strategy on a year-by-year basis. The higher the level of fund thus required to match the target income, the more the annuitant is exposed to the main threat to the efficacy of staggered vesting – poor investment returns and falling annuity rates.

So, what drives the level of the target fund? Primarily the annuity basis the retiree would select if the conventional annuity route were to be selected.

If that retiree would, in the normal run of events, select a single life annuity without guarantee, the income from a conventional annuity would be at its highest and, therefore, the attractions of a staggered vesting strategy might not be so great.

If on the other hand the retiree preferred a joint life annuity with a ten-year guarantee, the conventional annuity income would be much lower and so the target income for the staggered vesting strategy would be much lower. In these circumstances the staggered vesting strategy might appear much more attractive.

As a general rule, staggered vesting will prove much more attractive to retirees who want to provide the highest level of death benefits to a selected beneficiary. The further attractions of the staggered vesting strategy for these people include the flexibility of nomination of beneficiary or beneficiaries, including the ability to change the nomination of those beneficiaries (see later in this chapter).

FLEXIBILITY OF INCOME, UP TO AGE 75

The staggered vesting illustration indicates the assumed level of fund which has to be vested in each year to provide, overall, the annual target net income.

However, this target net income is only a notional target derived from the equivalent conventional annuity which could have been purchased at outset. In practice the annuitant may desire the flexibility to select in any given year a higher or lower income than that originally planned.

For many retirees this flexibility may be a significant attraction. Their other income, in retirement, might fluctuate from year to year, perhaps because of fluctuating consultancy income, infrequent maturity of investment policies, receipt of inheritances (however modest) or the final repayment of outstanding credit agreements, including mortgages. Conventional annuities lock in the annuitant to a predetermined level of annuity income for the rest of life. Even if an escalating pension is selected, this rate of escalation is impossible to change after the annuity payments have started.

It is vital to note that staggered vesting is not a new type of pension or annuity policy; it is simply a way of arranging 'ordinary' personal pension contracts in such a way as to make the 'staggering' of 'vesting' possible (i.e. through multiple policies or policy segments). A staggered vesting illustration (or 'quotation' as some providers call them, very misguidedly in the view of the author) is no more or less than a reasonably sophisticated spreadsheet computer program which illustrates what the retiree might be able to do if a number of assumptions (in particular fund growth and future annuity rates) materialize. The illustration does not say that the retiree *must* follow the plan, even if he or she *can* follow it.

ACCUMULATING NET INCOME FROM ANNUITIES PREVIOUSLY 'BOUGHT'

As each year of the staggered vesting strategy passes, more and more conventional annuities are purchased. The accumulating value of these annuities forms the minimum amount of income the retiree will receive in the following year (because each annuity is payable for the lifetime of the annuitant).

This increasing 'underpin' to the retiree's future income may be seen as advantageous in that it provides an increasing level of guarantees: if the staggered vesting strategy works favourably for only seven or eight years the member will have secured a series of guaranteed annuities providing income not much lower than the conventional annuity that could have been purchased at the outset.

However, a possible downside effect of this progressive purchase of conventional annuities is that it increasingly reduces the scope of flexibility of income levels: the minimum income increases each year while less investment fund is available. Thus typically both the minimum and maximum levels of income will tend towards convergence (i.e. the minimum level increases while the maximum level decreases).

CHOICE OF ANNUITY BASIS FOR EACH YEAR'S VESTED SEGMENTS

When it comes to the time(s) to buy a conventional annuity the choice arises as to the basis of the preferred annuity options, including whether to buy a level or escalating pension, whether to include a guarantee period, and so on.

Of particular interest is the decision as to whether or not to make provision for a surviving spouse or dependant within these annuities. As we have noted above, the staggered vesting strategy might be particularly attractive to retirees who would, through conventional annuity purchase, buy a joint life annuity. For these people we may assume that they therefore want to make provision for their spouse or dependant within staggered vesting and the assumption might therefore be that they will buy a joint life pension with each vested segment. This may, indeed, be advisable, but only in the light of the issues we now discuss in the next two sections.

DIRECTION OF DEATH BENEFITS

Financial provision for a surviving spouse, within a staggered vesting strategy, may not only be made through the purchase of joint life conventional annuities but also, perhaps even more importantly, the full value of the (unvested) fund is payable on death to the beneficiary of the member's choice. This will usually be payable as a lump sum free of liability to tax, although note the special position where the fund has been transferred from an occupational pension scheme.

Thus the total amount payable on the death of a retiree following the staggered vesting strategy is the total of:

a) the value of any spouse's or dependant's pension benefits provided from the previous conventional annuity purchases; plus
b) the value of any outstanding guarantee periods provided through previous conventional annuity purchase; plus
c) the value of the remaining – unvested – part of the fund.

Subject to the size of the remaining fund, therefore, it may be considered that it is not necessary to make provision for a spouse's pension through the conventional annuity purchases: the remaining fund might be more than sufficient to meet a survivor's needs.

However, note needs to be taken of the position of the surviving spouse when the member reaches the age of 75, as discussed below.

BUYING A SPOUSE'S PENSION AT AGE 75

No later than age 75 the retiree must vest all the personal pension policies or segments. In the last section we noted the commonly promoted strategy that annuity purchases prior to this time would be made on a single life basis only. However, if the retiree reaches age 75 with accumulated annuities all on a single life basis and still wishes to provide for a substantial surviving spouse's pension, he or she must note that the fund remaining at age 75 may not be enough to purchase a joint life annuity giving the spouse the level of benefits required.

A quick look at our earlier worked example illustrates this point. The notes at the foot of the example state that the conventional annuity quotation based upon outright purchase at age 60 made provision for a 50% spouse's pension (around £6,000 net per annum), but the conventional annuity purchases using the staggered vesting approach have all been completed on a single life basis. Looking at the projected level of the remaining fund at the end of each year we can see this never falls below £60,000. Given that this £60,000 will generally be payable tax free to the member's spouse (or nominated beneficiary), and that this could be used to buy, say, a purchased life annuity with a high capital content, the £6,000 net target spouse's annuity should be satisfied from this fund.

However, at the member's age 75 the remaining fund must be vested. According to our illustration this fund will be a little under £75,000: enough to provide a tax-free lump sum of £18,653 with a remaining further *single life* pension of a little under £5,000 per annum. Alternatively, a joint life pension could be bought at this time but, even on a 100% surviving spouse's pension basis, this would produce much less than the £6,000 target. Of course, the tax-free cash could be used to subsidize this shortfall but it has to be accepted that there is a very real risk that the full target level of spouse's pension may not be able to be met if in previous years only single life pensions have been bought.

Against this risk we can note that if spouse's pensions were to be bought each year as part of the conventional annuity purchases there may be significant *overprovision* for the spouse should the member die before reaching age 75 (when the value of the remaining fund is taken into account). Moreover, the purchase of joint life pensions would require more of the fund to be vested, each year, than the illustration currently shows: almost invariably indicating that the staggered vesting strategy would not work to the long-term financial benefit of the member. Finally, should the spouse die before the member reaches the age of 75 then all of the vested funds used to provide a spouse's pension will have proved wasted (unless, perhaps, the purchase was on the 'spouse at date of death' basis).

Overall, the fundamental concept of the staggered vesting strategy indicates the purchase of single life benefits only with acceptance of the possible risks to the financial provision for a spouse or dependant.

FUTURE ESTIMATES OF ANNUITY RATES

The net illustrated pension, bought by the vesting of successive segments of the fund, assumes that the underlying interest rates applicable to future annuities will remain at a certain assumed level. This assumption might well prove seriously and detrimentally wrong for one of two reasons: interest rates may fall, affecting annuity rates, or life expectancy assumptions may rise (causing annuity rates to fall), or both of these events may occur.

If annuity rates fall over the years then more of the remaining fund must be vested to provide the target level of net pension. This might not create an immediate problem in the early years of the strategy, but it is easy to envisage how quickly the fund could be depleted within only a small number of years of annuity rates falling much lower than the original assumptions.

Perhaps worse, if higher amounts of the fund have to be vested at a time when the investment performance of the fund is poor, the fund could be quickly wiped out altogether, leaving the retiree with only the conventional annuity income already purchased as retirement income for the rest of his or her life.

Against this prospect, however, let us not lose sight of the possibility that interest rates may rise above the rate assumed and, in particular if investment performance proves better than expected, the retiree's future financial position will be significantly enhanced as, indeed, will be that of the retiree's spouse or dependants.

INVESTMENT RETURN

This is almost certainly the most easily and commonly understood risk connected with the staggered vesting strategy although, as with annuity rate movements, the potential for volatility is arguably just as likely to be beneficial (good investment performance) as detrimental (poor performance).

As a very rough and ready example, if in the second year of our illustration the fund does not grow by 9% (as assumed), from £128,000 to £138,000, but falls by 30%, this would indicate a fund at the start of year 3 of only around £75,000. Vesting £28,000 or so of this in the third year leaves a fund of £47,000. If this fund falls by a further 30%, to a little over £30,000 then, with around £23,000 vesting in year 4, there will be very little fund remaining for vesting inn future years – even if investment performance recovers. If annuity rates are also falling at this time the situation becomes even more detrimental.

I would, though, strongly stress that it would be just as acceptable to show the equivalent figures for strong investment performance and rising annuity rates.

SUMMARY

In summary, retirees must be aware of these two primary risks (falling interest rates and poor investment performance) and should only enter into the staggered vesting strategy if the potential severity, as well as the potential benefits, of these risks is fully understood.

The enhanced flexibility and (usually) level of death benefits over conventional annuities will frequently override the investment and annuity rate considerations, especially for retirees who are in a poor state of health and/or whose spouse is in a poor state of health.

The eventual retirement income option decision will, as we continue to stress throughout this book, depend on the individual circumstances and requirements of each retiree.

8 Personal Pensions Drawdown

INTRODUCTION

After a couple of insurance companies had attempted to introduce pension drawdown contracts in late 1994, with mixed or questionable success, the Inland Revenue accepted the potential attractions of this new type of 'annuity' and enabled the widespread introduction of these contracts in mid-1995. Primarily, pension drawdown has been introduced to offer an alternative to the purchase of conventional annuities – giving retiring pension scheme members the opportunity to link their future retirement income to equity returns rather than gilt returns. Moreover, pension drawdown has further potential attractions for annuitants, including:

- potential lump-sum death benefit, even after retirement;
- greater flexibility and control over pension benefits paid to dependents, after the death of the scheme member;
- greater control over the level of retirement income, from year to year;
- deferral of annuity purchase, securing (hopefully) higher eventual rates because the annuitant is older;
- deferral of commitment to a particular annuity basis (e.g. spouse's pension, level of escalation, etc.);
- investment control, achieving (hopefully) better rates of return than fixed-interest gilts (on which conventional annuity incomes are based).

You may notice that many of these potential advantages are very similar to those claimed for phased retirement and, further, that many of the risks we identified in the last chapter with phased retirement also apply to pension drawdown, as we will explain throughout this chapter.

You should note that there are separate rules applying to personal pension drawdown and occupational pension drawdown – the former being the subject of this chapter and the latter being discussed in the (much shorter) next chapter.

WHAT IS PENSION DRAWDOWN?

There are two versions of drawdown arrangements, by far the most flexible being *personal pension drawdown*, and it this – much more common – version of drawdown that we shall be examining in this chapter. Pension drawdown is an alternative to the purchase of a conventional pension annuity at retirement for personal pension members, or those able and willing to transfer to a personal pension.

Firstly we shall look at the basic concept of personal pension drawdown and outline the main fundamental rules governing its operation. Later in the chapter we look much more closely at the key determinants of whether the drawdown strategy may be advantageous for a retiree, both initially and in future years, in particular:
- mortality drag and mortality gain; and
- interaction of interest rates and investment performance

HOW PENSION DRAWDOWN DIFFERS FROM THE PURCHASE OF A CONVENTIONAL PENSION ANNUITY

Traditionally, at retirement, members of many types of pension arrangement had to use the part of their accumulated fund (not taken as a tax-free lump sum) to buy an annuity from an insurance company. Certain options have to be decided upon at that time (such as the provision of a spouse's pension, whether the annuity should remain level throughout life or should escalate every year etc.) and cannot subsequently be changed.

By using the drawdown contract, by comparison, the scheme member retains control of his pension fund and does not immediately have to buy an annuity. Until such an annuity is bought the member periodically draws from the fund to, in effect, provide pension income.

LIMITS TO AMOUNT WITHDRAWN

An upper limit to the amount that may be withdrawn in a given year is imposed, broadly equivalent to the annuity the member could have bought from an insurance company, based on a level, single life, annuity (except in relation to a protected rights fund, which uses joint life rates, with escalation – appropriate to the restrictions on how protected rights benefits may be taken). There is also a minimum amount that can be withdrawn, being 35% of the upper limit.

The limit is set with reference to prevailing Government bond interest rates, with tables of limits published by the Government Actuaries Department (GAD).

An initial limit for a particular drawdown arrangement is established at the outset of the contract, and is affected by:

a) the size of the fund (GAD limits are expressed 'per £1,000 of fund');
b) prevailing long term interest rates (higher limits apply in times of higher interest rates, as may be expected because this would also be the time of higher annuity rates);
c) the age of the retiree (higher limits for older people);
d) the sex of the retiree (higher limits for males); and
e) whether the funds are protected rights.

This initial limit is set for three years, after which time a new GAD limit is set for the following three years. The level of this new limit will almost certainly be different from the initial limit because of a certain change (increase) in factor (c) and an almost certain change in factors (a) and (b).

INVESTMENT STRATEGY WITHIN A DRAWDOWN CONTRACT

A key factor in achieving the member's objectives will be the achievement of satisfactory returns in the fund from which the pension is drawn. Annuity rates are closely related to the yields on gilts, but in the long term equities have historically outperformed gilts. Account will need to be taken of the member's attitude towards investment risk which may be coloured by the degree to which the member is or will be reliant on the pension drawn from and eventually purchased from the personal pension fund.

Thus the individual who has significant other income, for example from other investments, may be willing to take a greater risk. There is a relationship also to the intended timescale of the income withdrawal. A greater exposure to equity-based risk may be more acceptable and indeed more appropriate where, for example, income withdrawal from the fund starts at the age of 50 as opposed to starting at the age of 70.

This arises out of the fact at the younger age it may be many years ahead before the annuity is finally purchased.

The investment risk factor makes it appropriate to review the level of income being drawn annually rather than simply wait for the required recalculation of the maximum amount that may be drawn in accordance with the then Government Actuary's Department Tables.

The main risk to those who opt to use the income withdrawal facility is that associated with remaining exposed to future investment risk. A prolonged period of poor investment returns can have disastrous consequences on the value of the remaining fund. To produce a return that is better than inflation, in particular after charges, the investment of the fund will generally need to be in assets other than cash and fixed-interest securities such as gilts, thus there will generally be at least some exposure to equities. Historically over any reasonable period of time equities have generated a better total return than that available from gilts.

POSSIBLE RESTRICTIONS ON THE INVESTMENT OF THE DRAWDOWN FUND

If the drawdown contract is provided by an insurance company the fund may be invested in one or more of that company's pension funds. However, many drawdown providers, including insurance companies, write the contract in conjunction with a self invested personal pension (SIPP), which gives a wider choice of investment opportunities.

There are restrictions. Most commonly SIPPs are used to invest in stocks and shares, unit trusts and investment trusts, and commercial property. They may not, however, lend money to the scheme member or a connected person. Nor can the SIPP make any transactions with the member (for example, buying shares held by the member). Investment in residential property is also not permitted.

WHAT HAPPENS, THEN, IF INTEREST RATES FALL BEFORE THE NEXT THREE-YEAR REVIEW?

The limit to the amount which may be withdrawn will also fall as a rate per £1,000 of fund. Thus if the value of the fund has remained level, or also fallen, the amount that the member may withdraw will be restricted to a lower level. Even if the fund has increased during that three-year period, the withdrawal limit may still fall if interest rates have fallen by a significant amount.

Thus a very real risk inherent in a drawdown contract is falling market interest rates, especially if they occur alongside a stagnant or falling fund value (which may occur either because of poor fund performance, or a high level of the fund being withdrawn, or a combination of the two factors).

THE ANNUITY RATE RISK ASSOCIATED WITH INCOME WITHDRAWAL

There is also the risk associated with the unknown level of annuity rates when the annuity is eventually purchased. Annuity rates increase with age. However because annuity rates are closely related to the yields available on medium-term and long-term gilts, they are subject to considerable variation over time. Thus the personal pension member who opts for income withdrawal is also taking the risk that annuity rates may, or may not, become more favourable over time.

Arguably, however, when interest rates fall the capital value of fixed-interest securities usually rise, as may the capital value of equities because a lower dividend yield will become acceptable to equity investors when the comparable income available from gilts is falling. This may result in a form of self-correcting protection, because the fall in annuity rates alongside a fall in gilt yields may be offset by the fact that the fund from which annuities are purchased may become larger – there is, of course, no guarantee of this.

TREATMENT OF THE DRAWDOWN FUND, FOLLOWING THE DEATH OF A MEMBER DURING THE DRAWDOWN PERIOD

There are four possible alternatives, depending on the relationship of the selected beneficiary to the deceased.

First, the beneficiary may purchase a conventional pension annuity in his or her own name.

Alternatively, the nominated beneficiary may continue the drawdown contract/strategy in his or her own name, but must buy a conventional pension annuity no later than his or her 75th birthday, or the date the deceased would have reached age 75, whichever is the earlier date.

A third option is for the beneficiary to take the drawdown fund as a lump sum, but this would then be subject to a special tax charge of 35%.

Finally, the beneficiary may simply leave the fund to accumulate, tax free, until then buying a conventional pension annuity no later than age 60.

The selection of preferred option is made following the death of the drawdown member; it does not have to be made when the arrangement is first established.

MORTALITY DRAG

There is a particular risk associated with pension drawdown, termed *mortality drag*. When annuities are purchased in the open market from a life office the actuary, given a large number of lives of a particular age, is able to calculate with considerable accuracy how many of that group will die from year to year by reference to mortality tables.

Those who live beyond their life expectancy benefit therefore from a mortality surplus that is in effect derived from those who die earlier than their life expectancy at outset. The deferral of annuity purchase leads to a loss of this mortality surplus in respect of the period of deferral, and this is the mortality drag. In other words, the longer the retiree lives the greater will be the loss of the mortality surplus while ever he or she remains outside of conventional annuities (i.e. while ever he or she remains within the drawdown environment). More discussion about this important point follows later.

CAN A DRAWDOWN MEMBER SELECT ANY DESIRED BENEFICIARY?

With conventional pension annuities a beneficiary must either be a legally married spouse or, otherwise, an individual who is financially dependent on the purchaser of the annuity. This restriction does not apply to drawdown, under which any individual may be nominated.

However, if the nominee is not the legally married spouse of the member, or otherwise financially dependent on him or her, then on death during the drawdown period that beneficiary must take the fund as a lump sum less 35% tax; the other options are not open.

Moreover, more than one beneficiary may be selected to receive any proportion of the total death benefits.

Finally, as regards the flexibility of death benefits within the drawdown contract, the nominated beneficiaries can be changed after the drawdown contract comes into force (but before the death of the member, of course).

This flexibility of death benefits is often cited (rightly, in the view of the author) as one of the main potential benefits offered by the drawdown contract over conventional annuities, giving the drawdown member the ability to change the nominated beneficiary at any time, perhaps particularly where:

- he (let us assume here that it is a man) becomes separated or divorced from his spouse at date of retirement (and may well, therefore, not want that person to receive death benefits); or
- he is not in a long-term relationship – whether or not legally married – and requires the flexibility to select and change beneficiaries in coming years; or
- he is happily married, but may want to instead select children or grandchildren to receive the death benefits for inheritance tax planning purposes; or
- his spouse may be in a poor state of health, so buying a joint life conventional annuity may prove bad value (part of the fund may be buying a benefit that is never paid); or
- he himself is in a poor state of health, and even the (limited) availability of impaired life annuities cannot give conventional annuity purchase anywhere near the same valuable death benefit as available under drawdown.

You may find it useful to refer back to Chapter 5 (definition of spouse and dependants) to give this important matter further consideration, contrasting in your mind conventional annuity restrictions with those applying to personal pension drawdown (and, for that matter, with staggered vesting).

CAN THE DRAWDOWN CONTRACT REMAIN IN FORCE INDEFINITELY?

No. By the member's age 75 a conventional pension annuity has to be purchased. Thus a drawdown member must hope that interest rates will not fall and remain low until this time.

Maximum retirement ages – proposals
At the time of writing (September 1999) it has become increasingly clear, and confirmed, that the Inland Revenue is seriously considering removing the upper age requirement for vesting. This would mean, on first sight, that a pension scheme member would never have to use an accumulated pension fund to buy an annuity; always, therefore, leaving the fund intact. You might not immediately see the ramifications of such a development, perhaps thinking that few people would be financially able to survive without recourse to the support of their pension fund. However, as we explain in this chapter, there may be many circumstances – not least for inheritance tax planning – where ad infinitum deferral of annuity purchase could prove highly attractive.

However, while the author hopes and believes that the upper age limit will be abolished in the near future, it is certain that the Inland Revenue will introduce conditions that prevent excesses of vesting deferral for largely, or purely, tax deferral purposes.

NORMAL MINIMUM PURCHASE PRICE

The size of the fund from which income is to be withdrawn is generally regarded as a highly relevant factor. Most providers do not allow for income withdrawal plans to be set up unless the pension fund is at least £100,000 after the tax-free cash sum has been taken. The main reason for this is the costs normally associated with the establishment and administration of income withdrawal plans – not only initially but also on an ongoing basis, monitoring and advising on such issues as investment strategy, interest-rate movements, selection of beneficiary, etc.

MORTALITY DRAG AND MORTALITY GAIN: REGULATORY GUIDANCE

From the very first days of pension drawdown financial services regulators have formally warned advisers they must take into account the impact of mortality drag when considering whether to recommend pension drawdown contracts.

Mortality drag is described in outline above, but in these next sections we look much closer at how mortality drag arises, its impact, and its overall influence on the retirement income options decision. We will then look at the (almost converse) principle or concept termed *mortality gain*.

THE PRINCIPLE OF MORTALITY DRAG

When a retiree purchases a pension annuity not only is the future level of income guaranteed but also the annuitant's benefit from a mortality subsidy. When the life office actuary is determining the level of income it calculates the probable future life expectancy of an individual for any given age. You do not have to be an actuary to understand that the older the individual is when he or she commences an annuity the shorter the future life expectancy. The mortality subsidy inherent in the annuity will increase the older the annuitant.

So what does this mean to the retiree who has chosen pension drawdown?

These retirees will not be entering into a pooled arrangement and consequently will not be benefiting from a mortality subsidy. As they are not benefiting from the subsidy they will have to achieve a rate of investment return over and above the interest rate used in the calculation of the annuity to match the level of income from the annuity. The interest rate will approximately equate to the yield on long-dated gilts. Accordingly the older the retiree when he or she commences pension drawdown the greater the subsidy loss and the higher the required investment return required to match the level of income from an annuity.

The following table shows the additional growth required by a drawdown fund over and above the annuity interest rate at various ages to match the conventional annuity, assuming interest rates remain unchanged.

(Note that these rates vary according to a number of factors, including the prevailing level of underlying interest rates and the charges imposed on pension drawdown contracts.)

Retiree Age	Additional Growth Required Over and Above Interest Rate %
50	0.34
55	0.60
60	1.05
65	1.84
66	2.02
67	2.22
68	2.44
69	2.69
70	2.96
71	3.26
72	3.58
73	3.94
74	4.34

A WORKED EXAMPLE OF MORTALITY DRAG, COURTESY OF THE FINANCIAL SERVICES REGULATORS (1995 EXAMPLE)

Let us consider a male aged 60 with an accumulated fund of £100,000 who after taking financial advice on the various retirement options available has decided the most suitable route for his personal and financial requirements is income drawdown.

The accumulated fund could have provided a level of income of £10,300 p.a. non-guaranteed and level in payment from a conventional annuity. The underlying interest rate of the annuity is 8.16%.

The retiree has decided to opt for the maximum income withdrawal of £10,300 from the income drawdown contract. Over the next three years the investment return achieved on the drawdown fund is 8.16% p.a., which is equal to the interest rate of the annuity. As the following table shows the value of the fund after three years is £91,900. But what fund value is required to produce a level of annuity of £10,300 which the retiree could have opted for at age 60 assuming that there has been no change in annuity rates?

The fund value required at age 63 needed to produce an annual annuity of £10,300 would be £94,500. A shortfall therefore exists between the actual fund value of £91,900 and the required fund value of £94,500. So what extra investment return is required above the achieved of 8.16%?

The total investment return over the three-year period would need to be 9.3% p.a. to provide a fund value of £94,500. This is a rate of return of approximately 1.1% p.a. above the underlying interest rate of the conventional annuity.

If we project forward to when the retiree is 75, the table shows an extra investment return required over the whole period of income withdrawal of 1.8% p.a.

Age	Fund £	Maximum Income Withdrawal £	Cost of Annuity £10,300 p.a.	Inv. Return % p.a.	Extra Return % p.a.
60	100,000	10,300	100,000–	–	
63	91,100	9,930	94,500	9.3	1.1
66	81,100	9,490	88,000	9.4	1.2
69	70,000	8,820	81,700	9.6	1.4
72	58,200	7,980	75,200	9.8	1.6
75	46,200	6,840	69,600	10.0	1.8

This extra rate of return results from those individuals who enter into a pension drawdown contract not benefiting from a pooled arrangement and not benefiting from a mortality subsidy.

The older the retiree when commencing income drawdown, the higher the real rate of return required and retirees will need to invest a higher portion of their retirement fund in equity/type investments, which may not correspond to the retiree's attitude to risk. To achieve a rate of return of 3% p.a. plus would require a speculative attitude to risk and would deter most pensioners from pension drawdown if they want to maximize their income in retirement.

The above table shows the investment return needed to match the level of income from an annuity, but many retirees decide to take a level of income less than that from an annuity. About 20% of individuals with income drawdown contracts take maximum income. For those retirees not taking maximum income the real rate of return required would be less because more of the retirement fund will be available for investment. Consequently the mortality issue becomes less of a risk the lower the level of income taken.

Advisers and retirees have to understand the inherent risks of mortality drag in connection with pension drawdown, but other factors need to be fully considered when assessing the overall mortality risk.

MORTALITY GAIN

The 'target' level of conventional annuity used in this early explanation of mortality drag was based on a single life annuity. It was not too long, though, before the regulators accepted that such a target figure might not (and, in fact, will not and is not) appropriate to every retiree. If an individual would elect for a surviving spouse's or dependant's pension within a conventional annuity, the target income would be much lower. Credit is being given to the attractions of pension drawdown for, in effect, not charging for death benefits; they are provided automatically, without charge.

There are many different ways of attempting to explain mortality gain but perhaps the simplest is to consider how conventional annuity rates are arrived at – primarily by combining underlying interest rates with mortality expectation.

Thus, while interest rates will determine how much income the insurance company can derive from investing the annuity purchase money, the retiree's life expectancy (mortality) will also be taken into account. If, for example, the underlying interest rate is 8%, the insurance company knows that it will receive £8,000 of income for every £100,000 it invests and can therefore afford to pay out this £8,000 (less, of course, charges and expenses).

However, the insurance company at this stage still has £100,000 of the retiree's money and it is a fundamental principle of pension annuities that, on the retiree's death, this money remains with the company. The insurance company therefore also costs into the annuity rate the return of this £100,000 to the retiree spread steadily over his or her remaining life – based on his normal life expectancy. But let us say that the life expectancy of this retiree is 10 years and he or she actually survives 15 years. Then, surely, the insurance company loses money having actuarially returned the retiree's original investment over only a 10-year period? This is true, but the insurance company will remain unperturbed because it will have other annuity retirees who die much earlier than their normal life expectancy predicted. These retirees who die early actuarially subsidize those who survive for a long time.

This effective cross-subsidy is true only within the conventional annuity market, whereas a drawdown retiree is, in this respect, 'on his own'. Inevitably, the longer he lives, the greater is the impact of this lost cross-subsidy or, put another way, the higher must be his investment return – thus mortality drag becomes more pronounced the greater the term of years the retiree survives within the drawdown strategy.

However, what was not recognized in the PIA document of 1995 (although recognized in a 1998 PIA document) is the concept of *mortality gain*. The 1995 document gives, as noted above, an income for the example retiree of £10,300. This is the GAD limit that is appropriate to a single life – that is, a retiree who buys an annuity to be paid throughout his or her own lifetime but which ceases entirely on death.

But what if the retiree had used the £100,000 fund to buy a joint life pension (or to be more technically correct, a surviving spouse's pension) via the conventional annuity route? Had he (or she) done so, the annuity level he could have purchased would have been significantly lower than the £10,300 for a single life pension: as an approximation, for a 100% spouse's pension he could have expected perhaps some 20% less income – around £8,300. Then, if he had entered into drawdown and taken not the maximum GAD limit (£10,300) but the lower amount of £8,300 (equivalent to the potential joint life pension) his fund would have fallen much slower than illustrated in the 1995 PIA document.

We can see then that the remaining fund at age 63 would be much higher than £91,000 (as illustrated in the mortality drag example) – perhaps in the region of £98,000. It can be calculated that the fund required to buy a conventional annuity of £8,300 at that first triennial review will be somewhat lower than the £98,000 actually remaining in the drawdown fund. Thus the retiree may then be in 'profit' and this 'profit' increases the longer the retiree remains within the drawdown contract. This has recently become known as mortality gain. Many actuaries contend, with some justification, that there is no such thing as mortality *gain* – the principle can do no more than represent a reduction in mortality *drag*. However, if one takes into account the actuarial value of personal pension drawdown death benefits in the event of the death of either the drawdown member or the spouse, or both, then it is possibly to identify a 'gain' in most cases, even if the actuaries would prefer not to call it 'mortality gain'.

Quite simply, mortality drag is a valid assessment of an individual who might ordinarily have bought a single life annuity, but decides instead to follow the drawdown strategy. Mortality gain may be a valid assessment of a retiree who would ordinarily buy a survivor's pension (joint life pension) – especially if the proportion of survivor's pension is high (say $2/3^{rds}$ or 100%).

Perhaps the simplest way to approach mortality gain is to consider that buying a joint life pension requires the retiree to forego up to around 20% of the income he or she could have bought on a single life basis or, putting it a different way, to use 20% of the fund to buy that survivor's pension. In the drawdown strategy the death benefits – almost invariably at least equivalent to the value of the survivor's pension via the conventional route – are 'free'. Thus 20% of the fund is 'saved' over the period of the drawdown contract and this 'saving' can be annualized to give the effective annual mortality gain.

ASSESSMENT OF THE IMPORTANCE, OR OTHERWISE, OF MORTALITY GAIN

How can these concepts of mortality gain and mortality loss be understood or appreciated by retirees? The answer is that they do not particularly need to be fully understood in great technical or actuarial depth, but the implications arising from these concepts do. Moreover the implications must be taken into account by the adviser in formulating any drawdown recommendation.

Quite simply, it would be useful and appropriate for a retiree to be asked (or ask himself, if acting without an adviser) at the outset what annuity basis he or she would ordinarily select if following the conventional route – primarily whether he (or she) would select a single life pension or a joint life pension and, if the latter, what proportion of his own pension he would choose to have paid to a survivor. The adviser can obtain an illustration from a conventional annuity provider on the retiree's required annuity basis and this level of annuity (lower if the joint basis is selected) will form the target income for a comparative drawdown illustration.

Given this target level of income, an insurance company will calculate the critical yield, which is the average annual growth rate required from the drawdown contract in order to match the level of annuity that would have been purchased down a conventional route.

Therefore, the critical yield will be considerably lower for a retiree who would have selected the joint life option than for a retiree who ordinarily would have selected the single life option – the difference in these critical yields being the difference between mortality drag and mortality gain.

As an example, illustrations were obtained from a leading pensions office at a time when the yield on long-dated gilts was around 5.7%. The critical yield for a drawdown contract for a retiree who ordinarily would have selected a single life pension via the conventional route was a shade under 8% – entirely to have been anticipated – this being around 2% over the prevailing long-dated gilt rate and also the level of mortality drag illustrated in the 1995 PIA document. The critical yield though for the joint life retiree (with 100% spouse's pension) and, consequently much lower target income, was a shade under 5% (again entirely to be anticipated as being the value of mortality gain).

MORTALITY GAIN – CONCLUSION

The messages from the illustrations are clear, not least with regard the probable investment strategies each retiree might have to follow if the drawdown route is likely to be profitable – the 'joint life' retiree can adopt a much more conservative or defensive investment risk profile than the 'single life' retiree who will almost certainly have to be invested largely or entirely in equities to have any reasonable expectation of a continuing high level of income from drawdown.

If any general conclusion is to be reached from this description of mortality gain, surely the message is that a drawdown strategy is much more likely to be profitable and beneficial for retirees who would have bought a survivor's pension via conventional annuity purchase than for those who would otherwise have purchased a single life annuity.

INTEREST RATES AND INVESTMENT PERFORMANCE: PENSION DRAWDOWN – TOLERANCE TO INTEREST RATE MOVEMENTS AND FUND PERFORMANCE

Much has been written over recent months and years about the effect, both historical and prospective, of a reduction in long-term interest rates on the benefits that may be taken from pension drawdown contracts. This account calls into question the claimed severity of such reductions.

Pension drawdown contracts, enabled by legislation in 1995 as an alternative to the purchase at retirement of a conventional annuity (often termed compulsory purchase annuity), offer the ability for a retiree to draw annual required income from an investment fund. The most obvious point to note is that the retiree retains control over the fund, the level of which, in turn, determines the level of withdrawals that may be made. This is most usually perceived as a much higher risk alternative to conventional annuities under which the annuity office guarantees the income for the remainder of the annuitant's life (and possibly also the remainder of his nominated dependant's life, if longer).

GOVERNMENT ACTUARY'S DEPARTMENT TABLES

On commencing a drawdown contract, the maximum withdrawals for the next three years are restricted according to tables drawn up by the Government Actuary's Department. Different tables exist for males and females and for protected rights and non-protected rights, the more widely used non-protected rights tables broadly representing a competitive single life level annuity at a given market interest rate. The interest rate used is the redemption yield on long-dated government bonds and the limit thereby expressed within the tables is the maximum withdrawal per £1,000 of fund at the start of the three-year period.

At the end of this and subsequent three-year periods, a new restriction is calculated and applied according to the size of the drawdown member's fund at that time and prevailing interest rates (i.e. long-dated gilt redemption yields). If the fund and interest rates have remained static over the three-year period, the member's GAD limit will increase because of his (three years) older age and, therefore, reduced remaining life expectancy.

THE MAIN RISKS ASSOCIATED WITH PENSION DRAWDOWN

The main risks for a drawdown member are poor investment performance (especially if the level of withdrawals are high) and falling interest rates – both of which have a negative effect on the level of maximum withdrawal. Indeed, noting that an annuity must be purchased no later than the age of 75, falling interest rates and a falling fund value could combine to mean that the eventual annuity purchased may be lower – perhaps significantly lower – than that which could have been purchased at outset, i.e. when the drawdown contract was first established. It is the interest-rate risk that has unfortunately been overlooked by some advisers in the past and is now attracting particular attention from some market commentators, journalists and regulators.

TOLERANCE TO INTEREST RATE MOVEMENTS

Let us look at an extract from GAD tables for males, non-protected rights:

	5%	6%	7%	8%	9%	10%
60	80	87	95	103	111	119
63	86	94	101	109	117	125
66	94	101	109	117	125	133
69	103	110	118	126	134	142
72	114	122	129	137	145	153
75*	128	136	143	151	159	167

* Note: GAD limits do not exist for age 75 or above because, by this age, a conventional annuity must have been purchased. The figures in this line are therefore notional figures simply to illustrate the likely annuity rates at that age and interest rate.

It can be clearly seen that if interest rates remain constant, the GAD limit increases with age – substantially so between the ages of 60 and 75, for example. However, there is a significant tolerance even if interest rates fall – noticeable particularly by looking at diagonal trends (from right to left).

Take, for example, a male aged 60 at outset, with interest rates at 10%. His GAD limit – broadly reflecting the annuity rate on the open market – is £119 per £1,000. If, three years later, interest rates have fallen to 9%, his GAD limit (at £117) would be barely changed: the fall in interest rates being almost entirely counterbalanced by the increase in the member's age. A fall greater than 1% during this period would, however, lead to a fall in the GAD limit per £1,000 of fund. If by the time the member reaches the second triennial review (at age 66), interest rates have fallen from 10% to 8% but the GAD limit will again show no movement (at £117). Thus over two three-year periods a tolerance to interest reductions of up to 2% can be identified with little fall in the GAD limit (although, of course, there remains the investment risk). It is next perhaps instructive to draw a straight line through the numbers noted in this paragraph and continue the line to age 75. The sequence can then be seen:

	Interest Rate	GAD Limit
60	10%	£119
63	9%	£117
66	8%	£117
69	7%	£118
72	6%	£122
75*	5%	£128

The trend can be clearly noted: that the member can tolerate interest falls of up to 1% in each three-year period with little or no loss in GAD limit (per £1,000 of fund). Indeed, the tolerance increases at older ages somewhat greater than 1% per period. This tolerance could also be described as 'cumulative' in that if interest rates do not fall for three periods the tolerance in the fourth period is 4%. Conversely, if interest rates fall 4% in the first period there will be an immediate reduction in the member's GAD limit but this reduction will not be permanent if interest rates then remain stable: within three more periods the GAD limit will have returned, more or less, to its original level – a trend towards 'the diagonal'.

These 'diagonal line trends' can be identified for both males and females, and at all ages and interest rates. Thus, from any interest rate starting point, the tolerance to interest rate falls is 1% in every three-year period, up to the time when an annuity must be purchased (age 75). This means that, to use a common example, a 60-year-old drawdown member can tolerate a 5% fall in interest rates by the time he or she reaches age 75 (obviously, this spanning

15 years: 5 three-year periods). This is particularly interesting at a time when interest rates are lower than 5%!

INVESTMENT RISK

Of course, all we have shown is the absence of a 'loss per £1,000 of fund' because of interest rates. It must be remembered that a fall in the member's fund would, nevertheless, result in a reduction if the fall happened at a time when interest rates were also falling.

Cross tolerances between interest rates and fund value
Reminding ourselves of the extract from GAD tables:

	5%	6%	7%	8%	9%	10%
60	80	87	95	103	111	119
63	86	94	101	109	117	125
66	94	101	109	117	125	133
69	103	110	118	126	134	142
72	114	122	129	137	145	153
75*	128	136	143	151	159	167

Continuing our earlier example of the 60-year-old male with interest rates at 10%, if interest rates remain unchanged by the time be reaches 75 his GAD limit/annuity rate would have increased from £119 per £1,000 to £167 per £1,000. Put another way, though, he could tolerate a fall in his fund to 119/167ths and still maintain the annuity buying power. Thus a fund of, say, £100,000 would have a GAD limit at age 60 of £11,900. If the fund fell to 119/167ths of £100,000 that gives a reduction to £71,257 which, at a GAD rate of £167 per £1,000 at age 75, would give an unchanged limit/annuity rate. This means that the fund could fall in value by almost 29% without reduction in the GAD limit/annuity buying power. We have thereby started to identify what might be termed 'cross-tolerances', which can be continued as follows. (It might be useful to check against the above tables how each calculation has arisen).

Male age 60 at outset with interest rates at 10%. GAD limit of £119 per £1,000.

Interest Rate at 75	Interest Rate Fall	Fund Tolerance Calculation	%	Fund Tolerance as % Loss
9%	1%	119/159	75.8	24.2
8%	2%	119/151	78.8	21.2
7%	3%	119/153	83.2	16.8
6%	4%	119/136	87.5	12.5
5%	5%	119/128	93.0	7.0

So, we are now able to specify that the member can tolerate, for example, a 3% fall in interest rates and a 16.8% fall in fund with no loss to the eventual annuity purchasing power. This is surely a more useful and professional alternative to simply recounting to the member or prospective member that there exists an interest rate and an investment risk.

A particular word of caution, though: GAD limits do not match market annuity rates exactly. Furthermore, annuity companies could reduce their annuity rates in future irrespective of any fall in interest rates – perhaps because of generally increasing life expectancy or because they find themselves with fewer annuity buyers in a poor state of health to subsidize those who are likely to live longer. Thus, care must be taken in presenting the certainty of a final assumed annuity rate.

PERSONAL PENSION DRAWDOWN – SUMMARY

It should be clear that personal pension drawdown strategy will be highly attractive for many retirees, in particular for the flexibility of income, the ability to direct one's own investment strategy for retirement income until age 75, the potential for increasing interest (annuity) rates and for the hugely more flexible provision of death benefits (over conventional annuity purchase).

Against these benefits, of course, must be recognized the potentially huge damage from poor investment performance (particularly if this occurs while the member is drawing down significant amounts of the fund in the early years), falling interest rates, and the high degree of monitoring (and, therefore, increased charges) required to make the drawdown strategy potentially profitable.

The implications of mortality drag and mortality gain must be particularly understood and taken into consideration.

Overall the eventual retirement income option decision will of course depend on the circumstances and requirements of the individual retiree but, without a doubt (certainly for larger funds) personal pension drawdown cannot be overlooked.

9 Flexible Annuities within Occupational Pension Schemes

INTRODUCTION

In Chapters 7 and 8 we looked at the availability of what might be termed 'flexible annuities' within the personal pension environment, noting that neither staggered vesting nor personal pension drawdown is available to members of occupational pensions unless they first transfer to a personal pensions (and then become subject to the possible restrictions noted in Chapter 2).

In this chapter we look at the two main types of flexible annuity strategy available to members of occupational pension scheme members – occupational drawdown and (with restricted eligibility) small self-administered scheme (SSAS) deferred annuity purchase.

OCCUPATIONAL DRAWDOWN – INTRODUCTION

Following proposals announced during 1999, the Inland Revenue advised that it was prepared, subject to agreement with all relevant bodies, to allow drawdown facilities for members of occupational pension schemes. The rules have now been published, on the face of it making occupational drawdown very similar to personal pension drawdown, but with some important differences.

In the next sections, therefore, we shall be outlining these rules. However, because of the similarity of most of the rules to personal pension drawdown, already discussed in Chapter 8, we shall particularly concentrate on the differences between the two types of arrangement rather than simply repeat whole chunks of the text from the previous chapter.

ELIGIBILITY TO OCCUPATIONAL DRAWDOWN

There is no obligation upon employers (or trustees) to offer a drawdown facility. The risks associated with drawdown can make it unsuitable for many members, even if the value of their pension fund is high enough, and anyone who wishes to use a drawdown facility needs to be able to understand the downside as well as the benefits. For example, understanding that future investment returns are important and why equity-related investment with its inherent risks is almost obligatory. With personal policies, there is normally an adviser explaining all the factors to be taken into account and reviewing the situation year by year. Who would take on this role with an occupational pension scheme? The trustees? Very unlikely, because they would have to be authorized to give such financial advice. With trustees' obligations and fears of repercussions against them if a disadvantage arises, trustees may well decide that the option will not be included in their scheme.

AGE LIMITS

A member is allowed to start taking benefits between age 50 and 75, whether or not actually retired.

LIMITS TO LEVELS OF WITHDRAWAL

The basis of income withdrawal is the same as for personal pensions, in respect of both minimum and maximum. That is, there is an upper limit by reference to Government Actuary Department (GAD) tables and a lower limit, being 35% of that upper limit.

DEATH OF THE DRAWDOWN MEMBER

On the member's death, the maximum lump-sum death benefit is limited to any guaranteed period pension commutation, as with conventional annuities.

This is a particular point of distinction with – the much more flexible – personal pension drawdown. With a personal pension drawdown the remaining fund less the 35% tax charge may be payable as a lump sum or, for legally married spouses and other financial dependants, other options are valuable for the treatment of the remaining drawdown fund.

This therefore means that, under occupational drawdown, if a member for whom there is no provision for a surviving spouse's pension to be payable dies soon after starting to take retirement benefits, it could well be the case that a substantial amount of the drawdown fund cannot be payable to the deceased's beneficiaries.

WHAT HAPPENS TO A SURPLUS FUND ON THE DEATH OF AN OCCUPATIONAL DRAWDOWN MEMBER?

The part of the fund that cannot be paid on the death of a drawdown annuitant remains within the fund or is paid to the pension scheme, therefore benefiting the remaining members of that scheme or the employer (if a scheme surplus is paid to the employer).

With pension drawdown, many retirees wish to draw income only as necessary, and ideally as little as possible so that the maximum amount of fund remains invested to benefit from (hoped for) attractive investment growth. The more that is taken out in the early years, the harder it is for the remaining fund to achieve the growth needed to provide the future pension required – not least to overcome the effects of mortality drag.

However, with occupational pension drawdown it is possible that if a member draws only a modest amount of income initially and the fund benefits from above average investment returns, when the member comes to have that remaining fund converted to an annuity at a later date, it is more than sufficient to provide the maximum benefits allowed within Inland Revenue rules. The excess fund is retained by the pension scheme.

This means that the member will have taken the investment risk (in that the fund might *not* have grown as much as required) and yet may not fully benefit from the investment upside in the same way that would have resulted from a personal pension drawdown arrangement.

This puts the member considering drawdown in an invidious position. If he or she draws too much he runs the risk of the fund becoming insufficient to meet his needs in subsequent years, and yet if he draws too little he may just be helping the pension fund anticipate a significant 'windfall profit'.

OCCUPATIONAL PENSION DRAWDOWN: THE TAX-FREE CASH CONUNDRUM

An added complication with occupational drawdown relates to the taking of tax-free cash at retirement. If the minimum amount of pension within GAD limits is taken (35% of the maximum allowed) and the maximum tax-free cash sum is calculated in relation to the pension taken in the first year, this may unduly influence the retiree to take a higher level of retirement income than he needs or wants.

OCCUPATIONAL DRAWDOWN COMPARED TO PERSONAL PENSION DRAWDOWN

In summary, the greater level and flexibility of death benefits allowed under personal pension arrangements makes occupational drawdown less attractive than personal pension drawdown for many individuals, especially where the 'tax-free cash conundrum' becomes a consideration. One might be tempted, then, to conclude that occupational pension scheme members would be better advised to transfer to a personal pension to obtain these preferential drawdown aspects.

However, it should not be forgotten that occupational pension scheme members may not be able to transfer to a personal pension (they might not be able to satisfy the maximum funding test) or may suffer other consequences of such a transfer – perhaps restricted availability of tax-free cash (restricted to no more than 25% of the pension fund).

SMALL SELF-ADMINISTERED SCHEMES (SSASs) – AN INTRODUCTION

There have, for many years longer than the availability of pension drawdown, been special rules relating to the availability of a type of flexible retirement income facility within SSASs

A small self-administered scheme (SSAS) is defined as a scheme with less than twelve members where 'some or all of the income or other assets are invested otherwise than in insurance company policies'.

A more complete definition of an SSAS is beyond the scope of this book. Here, we shall describe the options open to a retiring member from an SSAS, assuming that the scheme has met the conditions of being deemed to be an SSAS.

Mostly, then, these schemes are established for a small number of employees – almost invariably senior executives and directors (most or all of whom are also shareholders) – who seek greater flexibility of investment opportunities than the collective funds offered by insurance companies.

Typical investments within an SSAS include loans to the employer company that established the SSAS and the purchase of commercial property which the company then occupies part or all of.

The special rules to enable the deferral of annuity purchase for SSASs were introduced primarily to give these schemes enough time, after the retirement of a scheme member, to liquidate enough scheme assets to pay a pension without having to 'panic sell' those assets at knock-down prices.

BENEFITS FROM AN SSAS – INTRODUCTION TO SSAS DEFERRED ANNUITY PURCHASE ('SSAS DRAWDOWN')

Although the SSAS may simply purchase the members pension benefits by purchasing compulsory purchase annuities in the open market, an alternative is to drawdown the member's pension from the SSAS fund itself.

The initial rules permitted the deferral of annuity purchase for up to five years following retirement of a scheme member but, since February 1994, it has been possible for an SSAS to pay pension benefits from the fund in respect of the member, although an annuity for the member must be purchased by the age of 75. This, as noted above, may be of particular relevance where part of the fund is held in relatively illiquid investments such as commercial property, therefore giving the trustees greater flexibility in terms of managing the timing of the disposal of such assets.

THE RULES SURROUNDING DRAWDOWN FROM AN SSAS

The conditions laid down in this regard are as follows:
- The pension benefits for a member as well as any pension benefit for a dependent may be drawn from a fund in this way. In this regard the dependant's pension must be purchased by the earlier of the date at which the deceased member would have reached age 75 or the attainment of age 75 by the dependant.
- Part of the annuity may be purchased following retirement and prior to the age of 75, but in any event the total annuity must have been purchased by that time.
- Drawdown is permitted if the income derived is within 10% of the open market option annuity that would have been possible when the

member retired, having taken account of any provision for dependant's benefits.

These rules are very different and far more flexible than those that preceded them, but the rules of the SSAS have to have been amended to permit this facility before it can be put into operation.

THE PROVISION OF DEATH IN SERVICE BENEFITS

The SSAS may of course be used to provide benefits payable as lump sum and pension up to the usual limits applicable to occupational pension schemes. However, until the scheme is well established, with substantial funds, the SSAS will not generally be in a position to afford the provision of such a liability out of the member's share of the fund should death occur during the drawdown period. Thus the Ttrustees will normally choose to insure this liability.

DRAWING INCOME FROM THE SSAS FUND

Drawdown of benefits pre-February 1994
Although the SSAS may simply purchase the member's pension benefits by purchasing compulsory purchase annuities in the open market from an insurance company, an alternative is to simply drawdown the member's pension from the SSAS fund itself.

Until February 1994 the SSAS, if the member's pension was not purchased outright, was permitted as an alternative to pay members' pensions from the scheme assets for a period of up to five years after a member's retirement and within this period the member's pension benefits had to be purchased by way of a pension annuity from a life office. The main advantage of this facility was that if the scheme trustees perceived that annuity rates were relatively low at the time that benefits commenced to be paid, the annuity purchase could be delayed to a time when the trustees found annuity rates to be more attractive.

Drawdown of benefits after February 1994

With effect from 4 February 1994, it became possible for the pension purchase to be deferred for as long as to the member reaching the age of 75. In relation to SSASs established before 5 August 1994, the ability to defer payment to up to age 75 may be used so long as the rules have been amended to allow for this facility or otherwise the five-year maximum period as described in the last paragraph will continue to be applicable. Similarly, in relation to schemes set up on or after 5 August 1994, the ability to defer purchase of benefit to age 75 at the latest is possible only if the rules of the scheme permit.

New rules in relation to drawing pension from the fund have therefore been possible for SSASs since February 1994 and they allow the SSAS to pay pension benefits from the fund in respect of the retiring member where a pension annuity for the member must be purchased by the time he or she reaches the age of 75.

SSAS INVESTMENTS DURING DRAWDOWN

The following provisions apply:

- Investments within the SSAS may continue in land and property while income is being drawn down but arrangements must be in place for there to be liquid assets in the fund to enable the annuity purchase between the age of 70 and 75.
- No additional loan to the employer, or any purchase of shares in the sponsoring company, may be effected during the time when withdrawals are being taken in this way, in relation to the assets of the SSAS that appertain to the member where drawdown is taking place.
- The SSAS is restricted in its borrowing powers in that the member's share of the fund is excluded from the value in the calculation of the relevant limits.

ACTUARIAL CERTIFICATION

It should be borne in mind that so far as the PSO is concerned the facility to defer the purchase of the member's benefit is for the purpose of giving SSAS trustees greater flexibility in determining the best time to purchase the member's benefit by way of an annuity from an insurance company. It is expected therefore that the relative attraction of continuing the drawdown as compared to buying a pension annuity is kept under review. This matter ought to be considered at trustees meetings and whenever there are market changes occurring that may reasonably result in an expectation of a rise in annuity rates.

More formally, the PSO requires that the scheme actuary certifies that the amount of pension being drawn down bears in mind any future requirement to purchase dependant's pensions and considers the value of the fund that has been set aside, that is notionally earmarked for the purposes of providing members' benefits. The actuarial certification must compare the pension being drawn down from that which could be secured on the open market and a gap of greater than 10% must be explained to the PSO. The actuary's certificate is provided to the PSO alongside the triennial actuarial valuation following the start of drawdown, but a certificate may be required earlier on request by the Pensions Schemes Office. Subsequent certification should be incorporated within the usual 3-yearly actuarial valuation of the scheme.

THE BENEFIT OF ANNUITY PURCHASE DEFERRAL

The attractions of annuity purchase deferral will be clear from the above. Not only can favourable annuity rates be awaited but investment flexibility can be maintained, important perhaps where a commercial property is the main asset of the fund.

Given that benefits may be taken from as early as the member reaching age 50, it is clear that drawdown could continue for up to 25 years.

The rules are very different and far more flexible than those that preceded them, but the rules of the SSAS must permit this facility before it can be put into operation. However, it should be obvious that the SSAS drawdown rules are much less flexible than those for occupational drawdown.

In common with occupational drawdown, it should be noted that 'surplus' SSAS drawdown funds following the death of the member or following the eventual purchase of the member's annuity at age 75 is retained within the scheme, obviously for the benefit of the remaining members of the scheme.

SUMMARY

It may be expected that SSAS drawdown will become less and less used for SSAS members who are attracted by the additional flexibility of occupational pension drawdown, and indeed a trend in this direction appears certain. However, the additional flexibility for the member will generally mean additional administration and monitoring by the scheme which, therefore, might be reluctant to agree to offer occupational drawdown as a facility. Against this, if the scheme allows a member to draw only a small proportion of the possible annual income (as low as 35%) then, arguably, the scheme might be inclined to agree to offer occupational pension scheme withdrawal with an increased opportunity of a future windfall profit to the scheme, as discussed above.

Finally, note that although SSAS members may have the choice between SSAS drawdown and occupational pension drawdown, members of non-SSAS occupational schemes may not be granted the availability of SSAS drawdown (not that they would want it anyway!). All members have the option to transfer to personal pension (subject to the maximum funding check) to gain access to personal pension drawdown or staggered vesting.

10 Comparative Factors in Retirement Options

INTRODUCTION

This chapter is designed to help to bring together a summary of the main comparative factors in determining which annuity income option, or combination of options, may be most suitable for retirees in different circumstances and with different priorities.

We have, through this book, looked at:

- conventional (guaranteed) annuities;
- with profit and unit-linked annuities;
- staggered vesting;
- personal pension drawdown;
- occupational pension drawdown;
- SSAS deferred annuity purchase.

For all of these annuity options we have looked at a number of comparative factors, these including, in particular:

- eligibility
- availability of a tax-free lump sum;
- possible restrictions on benefits;
- investment risk to the annuitant;
- guarantees to future level of annuity income;
- potential for future growth in income;
- flexibility of retirement income;
- death benefits.

We now want to consider each of these main factors for each of the different retirement income options. This will be done only briefly, and in note form, because we are doing no more than summarizing the more detailed discussion elsewhere in this book. Thus this aide-memoir chapter should be cross-referenced to the relevant text in the main book if you are uncertain on any issues.

CONVENTIONAL (GUARANTEED) ANNUITIES

Eligibility
Any pension scheme member reaching the minimum age to draw benefits. This might sound obvious, but you will note later that certain other options are available only to members of certain types of pension scheme.

Availability of tax-free lump sum
This depends on the type of pension scheme from which the annuity purchase monies arise: personal pension, retirement annuity contracts, occupational schemes and FSAVCs, to compile not an exhaustive list, all have different rules. The part of the fund that cannot be taken as a lump sum must be used to purchase an annuity.

Possible restrictions on retirement benefits
There are possible restrictions on the level of benefit payable from annuities where the money arises from an occupational pension scheme. Further restrictions apply, in these instances, to benefits that may be payable to the spouse or legal dependants following the death of a scheme member. Maximum rate of escalation is applied to the pension in payment.

Investment risk to the annuitant
None. All the investment risk in securing the guaranteed annuity is borne by the annuity provider.

Guarantees to future level of annuity income
Absolute guarantees. Fluctuations in future investment performance or interest rates does not affect the annuitant. The only conventional annuity with reduced guarantees in this respect are index-linked annuities: the level of future increases

depends on the level of future price inflation.

Potential for future growth in income
None, unless an escalating pension is selected.

Flexibility of Retirement Income
None; the level of future income is determined at outset and cannot be changed.

Death benefits
These depend on the annuity options selected at outset but, once selected, cannot be changed. Primarily death benefits can be provided by including a guarantee period and/or a surviving spouse's or dependant's pension. No lump-sum benefit may be paid, though, except by commutation of the remaining guarantee where death occurs within the guarantee period.

WITH PROFIT AND UNIT-LINKED ANNUITIES

Eligibility
As for conventional annuities, although some product providers may restrict eligibility to, say, personal pension policyholders only.

Availability of tax-free lump sum
As for conventional annuities.

Possible restrictions on benefits
As for conventional annuities.

Investment risk to the annuitant
Potentially high risk, depending on the assumptions made at the outset of the contract and the investment performance of the selected funds. The higher the level of assumed growth the higher will be the starting pension but the potential for future growth is restricted and there is a very real potential for income to fall in future years. Selection of a low assumed growth rate increases the potential for future increases in the annuity payments and reduces or

eliminates the risk of a reduction in those payments, but the starting level of pension will be lower.

Guarantees to future level of annuity income
Generally none for unit-linked annuities because the income will depend on the fluctuating investment performance of the underlying funds. With profit annuities enjoy more certainty but the level of this certainty depends on the assumptions made at outset (see above) compared with the actual level of bonuses declared each year.

Potential for future growth in income
Depends on investment performance and assumptions made at outset (see above).

Flexibility of retirement ncome
None; the level of future income depends entirely on the investment performance of the underlying investments, with no discretion given to the annuitant.

Death benefits
These must be selected at outset and cannot subsequently be changed. Therefore, the same as for conventional annuities.

STAGGERED VESTING

Eligibility
Only members of personal pensions and retirement annuity contracts, although for the latter members the purchase of the annuity will usually involve a transfer to a personal pension. Members of occupational pension schemes may usually transfer to a personal pension to gain eligibility, but then the level of tax-free cash, and death benefits, will be restricted.

Availability of tax-free lump sum
Technically available but, in practice, the tax-free lump sum is used, in effect, to subsidize regular annual income. Thus the tax-free cash is not available for

'windfall spending' as would ordinarily be the case. Tax-free cash may in any event be restricted if the funds have been transferred from an occupational pension scheme.

Possible restrictions to benefits
Because these are personal pensions there are no restrictions to benefits unless the fund has been transferred from an occupational pension scheme, in which case there may be restrictions on the level of tax-free cash and also on the lump-sum death benefit.

Investment risk to the annuitant
At the outset the investment risk is very high, although dependant on the investment strategy selected. At this time the bulk of the value is held within the investment fund with only a relatively small proportion used to buy a conventional annuity. However, as the years progress more and more of the fund is used to buy conventional annuities and so the level of future investment risk falls.

Guarantees to future level of annuity income
Initially there are no guarantees, but then guarantees start to arise as conventional annuities are bought on a year-by-year basis. As the years pass, so more guaranteed annuities are bought: by the end of the seventh or eighth year of the strategy the guarantees may be more than 75% of the initial target level of income.

Potential for future growth in income
No potential on the vested segments; the potential for future increases in income depends on the investment performance of the unvested part of the fund, i.e. the part of the fund left to accumulate after each year's segment is vested.

Flexibility of retirement income
Initially there is great flexibility of the level of income that may be taken, if we define 'income' to include the tax-free cash from the vested part of each segment. Of course, in the first year if all the fund is vested the 'income' includes the full amount of the tax-free cash sum plus the residual annuity. So, in that first year there is flexibility up to that point, but from as little as 'no

income' because there is no requirement to vest even a single segment.

However, each year's vested segments buy conventional annuities and the total income from all of these vested segments then becomes the minimum amount of income that may be taken in the following year – this being the level of income payable to the annuitant even if no further segments are vested. Thus the flexibility of the staggered vesting strategy reduces over the years as the minimum amount increases (vested segments) and the maximum amount decreases (remaining – unvested – fund).

Death benefits
On the vested segments the death benefits are exactly the same as for conventional annuities generally. For the unvested segments, this remaining fund is payable in full, usually as a lump sum, to the member's nominated beneficiary or his or her estate (depending on the wording of the pension contract). Note the possible restrictions where the fund was transferred to a personal pension from an occupational pension scheme.

PERSONAL PENSION DRAWDOWN

Eligibility
As for staggered vesting: only personal pension policyholders.

Availability of tax-free lump sum
Up to 25% of the fund, decided at the time the drawdown contract comes into force. May be restricted if the fund was transferred from an occupational pension scheme.

Possible restrictions on retirement benefits
None, for the scheme member. Spouse's benefits restricted to not be able to exceed the maximum pension the member could enjoy.

Investment risk to the annuitant
Very high, although depending on the selected investment strategy. The whole of the fund remains invested throughout the drawdown period with (usually)

no purchase of guaranteed (conventional) annuities in the meantime (unlike staggered vesting).

Guarantees to future level of annuity income
No guarantees until the fund is used to buy a conventional annuity: by the age of 75 at the latest.

Potential for future growth in income
Great potential for future growth in income, but this depends, prior to conventional annuity purchase, on the investment performance of the fund. At the date of annuity purchase the previous investment performance, together with the underlying annuity interest rate, will determine the future level of retirement income.

Flexibility of retirement income
Flexibility between the upper limit set by GAD, and the lower limit being 35% of the upper limit. Income level may be changed frequently between these limits. No flexibility after the age of 75 because a conventional annuity has to be bought by this time.

Death benefits
Legally married spouse and financial dependants have four main options, one of which is to take the whole fund as a lump sum, less tax at 35%. Beneficiaries not falling within these categories have no options: they must take the whole of the fund as a lump sum (less this special 35% tax). Lump-sum death benefit may be restricted to ensure that the potential pension for the beneficiary does not exceed the maximum pension the deceased could have received. Where the fund has been transferred from an occupational pension scheme there may be further limits.

OCCUPATIONAL PENSION DRAWDOWN;

Eligibility
Members of an occupational pension scheme who have agreed to make this

facility available (expected to be relatively few).

Availability of tax-free lump sum
Normal Inland Revenue maxima for occupational pension schemes generally.

Possible restrictions to benefits
Normal Inland Revenue maxima apply.

Investment risk to the annuitant
As for personal pension drawdown.

Guarantees to future level of annuity income
As for personal pension drawdown.

Potential for future growth in income
As for personal pension drawdown, but noting the overriding limit imposed by Inland Revenue maximum benefits.

Flexibility of retirement income
As for personal pension drawdown.

Death benefits
As for conventional annuities, with any surplus fund remaining in the scheme for the benefit of remaining members (or refund to the employer).

SSAS DEFERRED ANNUITY PURCHASE.

Eligibility
Members of SSASs only. Other occupational scheme members are not eligible.

Availability of tax-free lump sum
Normal Inland Revenue maxima apply.

Possible restrictions to benefits
Normal Inland Revenue maxima apply.

Investment risk to the annuitant
As for personal pension drawdown.

Guarantees to future level of annuity income
As for personal pension drawdown.

Potential for future growth in income
As for occupational pension drawdown.

Flexibility of retirement income
Relatively little flexibility: within 10% of comparative conventional annuity, reviewed every three years. More flexible than conventional annuities but much less flexible than personal or occupational drawdown.

Death benefits
As for occupational pension drawdown.

SUMMARY

In conclusion, from the above summary outlines and the supporting explanations throughout the book, the most appropriate course of action for a retiree can be established, depending on the relative importance he or she attaches to each of the main features and factors noted above.

Appendix 1: Inland Revenue Rules Relating to Maximum Benefits for Service of less than 40 years with an Employer

As stated in Chapter 3, the rules relating to members with less than 40 years of service by normal retirement date are extremely complex and are explained below.

The rules applicable depend upon the date on which a member joined his or her occupational pension scheme. For this purpose there are three categories of membership as follows:

- Pre-1987 members – pre-1987 benefits are allowed for schemes that were set up before 17 March 1987 in respect of members who joined before the same date.
- to 1989 members – benefits under this regime are relevant for scheme members who joined on or after 17 March 1987 and before 14 March 1989.
- Post-1989 members – this regime applies to individuals who joined a scheme set up on or after 14 March 1989 or who joined a scheme after 1 June 1989 if the scheme was set up before 14 March 1989.

In some circumstances it may be beneficial for a pre-1987 member or a 1987 to 1989 member to choose to be treated under the post-1989 regime.

A further category of members is those with continued rights. These are members who, although they joined the scheme in the period of time relevant to the 1987–1989 or post 1989 regime, qualify for treatment under the pre-1987 or 1987 to 1989 rules.

Maximum pension benefits for pre-1987 members

Under the pre-1987 regime a maximum pension of two-thirds final salary is allowed so long as at least 10 years service has been completed with the employer at normal retirement date. This includes the pension value of any tax-free lump sum. Benefits in excess of basic pension benefits (that is one sixtieth of final salary in respect of each year of service) can be provided only when more than 5 years service has been completed.

The scale of maximum pension benefits under this regime is known as the accelerated or uplifted scale, and is operational in accordance with the table below:

Years of service to normal retirement age	Maximum pension as a fraction of final salary
1-5	1/60 for each year
6	8/60
7	16/60
8	24/60
9	32/60
10	40/60

Fractions of a year may be interpolated into this scale.

When this accelerated scale or uplifted scale is used, retained benefits (See Appendix 3) must be taken into account. This means that other than where the basic benefit applies, the sum of the pension from the scheme of the current employer and the pension value of any retained benefits may not exceed 2/3rds of final salary. This includes the pension value of any tax-free lump sum.

Maximum pension benefits for 1987–1989 members

Following the provisions of the 1987 Finance Act the maximum pension that could be provided for a member joining the scheme on or after 17 March 1987 was amended to 1/30 final remuneration in respect of each year of service up to normal retirement date, with a maximum of 20 years to count. So under this regime, 20 years service has to be completed (an increase over the ten years under the earlier regime), as a minimum for the member to be entitled to a maximum pension benefit of two-thirds of final pay.

Again, if this approach is adopted retained benefits from schemes of previous employers must be taken into account. Note again that other than where the basic benefit applies, the sum of the pension from the scheme of the current employer and retained benefits may not exceed an overall maximum of 2/3rds of final salary. This includes the pension value of any tax-free lump sum.

Maximum pension benefits for post-1989 members

The relevant provisions were introduced in the Finance Act 1989. Under this regime it remains the case that a two thirds maximum pension can be achieved only after 20 years service on the basis of 1/30 final remuneration earned in respect of each year of service. This again includes the pension value of any tax-free lump sum. This maximum benefit may be provided at any age between 50 and 70 once 20 years service has been completed.

This regime is subject to the earnings cap mentioned in Chapter 3.

Maximum tax-free cash sum benefits for pre-1987 members

These members are subject to a provision where the maximum tax-free cash sum of 1.5 times final remuneration is allowed after 20 years service under what is referred to as the uplifted 80ths scale, otherwise once again sometimes referred to as the accelerated accrual basis. For service of less than 20 years, maximum tax-free cash benefits accrue in accordance with the table below:

Years of service to normal retirement age	Maximum tax-free cash as a fraction of final salary
1-8	3/80 for each year
9	30/80
10	36/80
11	42/80
12	48/80
13	54/80
14	63/80
15	72/80
16	81/80
17	90/80
18	99/80
19	108/80
20	120/80

Fractions of a year may be interpolated into this scale.

As with enhanced pension benefits, where the uplifted scale is being used retained benefits arising out of the membership of previous pension schemes must be taken account of. Therefore, where other than the basic tax-free cash benefit is being provided, the tax-free cash sum together with any retained cash benefits may not exceed 1.5 times remuneration.

A major advantage of the pre-1987 regime is that the maximum tax-free cash benefit in accordance with the above scale could be taken in isolation from the pension benefit. So it was possible, where 20 years service had been completed, for a benefit of 1.5 times final salary to be provided as a tax-free lump sum without any pension benefit at all. This seemed to be at odds with the basic rule that the cash is provided by way of giving up pension, if as a consequence there was no pension remaining.

Maximum tax-free cash sum benefits for 1987–1989 members

Under this regime it became no longer possible for the tax-free cash sum to be provided as a benefit in isolation using the uplifted 80ths scale. However a tax-free cash sum using the basic 3/80ths rule relative to actual years of service could still be provided on a stand-alone basis as described above. As an example, someone with 10 years of service could have a tax-free cash sum, without any pension at all, of ten times 3/80ths of final salary. If they wished to have a higher tax-free cash sum by using the accelerated 80ths option, then the scheme would have to be providing a pension of more than one sixtieth for each year of service. In this example it means that relative to the service of ten years, of more than 10/60ths, and the additional lump sum that could be obtained would depend upon the level of additional pension being provided.

This is the most complex of the three regimes as regards calculation of the maximum lump sum that the revenue will allow to be provided.

There is a standard formula to be used for calculation purposes, which is given below:

$$\text{Maximum tax free cash allowable} = \frac{(a-b) \times (d-e)}{(c-b)} + e$$

where

- $a =$ scheme pension being provided before any commutation for lump sum or allocation for widows/widowers/dependants' benefits
- $b =$ $1/60^{th}$ of final salary for each year of service with the employer before any deductions as in 'a'
- $c =$ $1/30^{th}$ of final salary for each year of service with the employer before any deductions as in 'a'
- $d =$ the maximum retirement lump sum using the accelerated table factors for a pre-87 scheme
- $e =$ the retirement lump sum using the $3/80^{th}$ of final salary for each year of actual service with the employer, up to 40 years

Restriction on tax-free cash

Other than where just the basic tax free benefit is provided the tax free cash sum together with any retained cash benefits may not exceed 1.5 times remuneration and is further restricted by a maximum remuneration of £100,000 applied for this purpose. Thus under this regime the maximum tax-free cash sum using the uplifted benefits rule became subject to an overall limit of £150,000.

Maximum tax-free cash sum benefits for post-1989 members

After the provisions of the Finance Act 1989 was introduced the maximum permissible tax-free cash sum was (thankfully!) simplified so as to be the greater of:
- 3/80ths of final remuneration in respect of each year of service – maximum of 40 years to count (i.e. the basic tax-free cash sum) plus any retained benefits; or
- 2.25 x the pension benefit before being commuted and before any reduction applied to purchase any spouse's or other dependant's benefits.

Other than where just the basic cash sum benefit is provided, the tax-free cash sum together with any retained cash benefits may not exceed 1.5 times final remuneration.

The earnings cap referred to with regard to pension benefits under this regime also applies, further restricting therefore the maximum possible value of the tax-free cash sum.

Example:

John Jones has been employed by the ABC Company for 15 years and is in an approved scheme. His salary at retirement is £30,000 p.a. His maximum benefits will be dependent upon when the scheme commenced:

If Pre-1987 – using the uplifted 60ths rule his maximum pension will be 40/60ths of final earnings, £20,000 p.a. He can forego some, or even as much as 100%, of this pension to withdraw maximum cash under the uplifted 80ths rule of 72/80ths, £27,000.

If 1987 to 1989 - his maximum pension is a strict 1/30th for each year of service and it will amount to 15/30ths or £15,000 p.a. He can withdraw tax-free cash up to 3/80ths for each year, 45/80ths, or £16,875. He can only withdraw excess above this up to a maximum of 72/80ths, or £27,000 as for a pre-1987 scheme, provided that the remaining pension that can be provided before commutation is £15,000.

Maximum tax free cash =

$$\frac{(15,000 - 7,500) \times (27,000 - 16,875)}{(15,000 - 7,500)} + 16,875 = £27,000$$

It can be seen from this that if the actual pension being provided by his scheme is less than £15,000 that the allowable lump sum will be lower. If Post 89 – his maximum pension is 1/30th for each year of service, 15/30ths, or £15,000 p.a. Under the 3/80ths rule his maximum tax-free cash is 45/80ths of £30,000 amounting to £16,875. Taking 2.25 times the pension before commutation (2.25 times £15,000) gives £33,750, a higher cash sum figure.

Appendix 2: Inland Revenue Rules Relating to Maximum Benefits for Early Retirement when less than 40 years Service

As stated in Chapter 3, the rules relating to early leavers and maximum benefits are extremely complex and are explained below. As mentioned in Chapter 3 the rules relating to early leavers on grounds of ill-health are based on the service that could have been achieved by normal retirement age and, in those circumstances, Appendix 1 is more relevant.

Pre-1987 members and 1987–1989 regime members

With regard to pre-1987 members and 1987-1989 regime members, an alternative to the basic benefits basis is allowed which may produce a greater figure.

For these regimes the following formulae may be used:

$N / NS \times P$ for pension benefits and
$N / NS \times LS$ for lump-sum benefits.

Under the above formulae:
$N =$ no. of years service completed to the actual date of early retirement.
$NS =$ no. of years service that would have been completed had retirement taken place at normal retirement date.
$P =$ maximum approvable pension that would have applied at normal retirement date based on final remuneration at the date of early retirement with any retained benefits deducted. Note it is at this

stage that any retained benefits are taken off. (See Appendix 3)
LS = maximum lump sum that would have applied at normal retirement date based upon final remuneration at the date of early retirement with any retained benefits deducted.

Post-1989 regime members

In respect of post-1989 regime members the calculation of maximum early retirement pension benefits is more straightforward. As an alternative to the basic n/60ths formula described above (but where appropriate applied to capped earnings and plus any retained benefits), a maximum of 1/30th of (capped) final salary may be allowed in respect of each year of service completed to the date of early retirement, but note that with the addition of any retained benefits an overall benefit limit of 2/3rds of (capped) final remuneration applies.

So where the uplifted scale (i.e. n/30ths rule) is applied retained benefits may be added in but the total benefit resulting is subject to an overall maximum of two-thirds of final remuneration at the date of early retirement and subject to the earnings cap.

With regard to the maximum tax-free cash sum applicable under this regime, the greater of the basic 3n/80ths rule applies — (based where applicable on capped earnings and with the addition of retained benefits and subject to no overall limit) or 2.25 times the scheme pension payable before commutation and any allocation for spouse's or dependants' benefits. However an overall maximum again applies of 1.5 times final remuneration (capped where appropriate) including any retained benefits.

Example:

John Jones has been employed by the ABC Company for 15 years and is in an approved money purchase scheme. He is taking early retirement at the age of 55, compared to his scheme normal retirement date of 65. His salary at retirement is £30,000 p.a.

His maximum benefits will be dependent upon when the scheme commenced:

If Pre-1987– Using the uplifted 60ths rule his maximum pension would have been 40/60ths of final earnings, £20,000 p.a. His maximum pension based on the formula above would be 15/25 times £20,000, equal to £12,000. Using the accelerated factors, had he continued to normal retirement date then under the uplifted 80ths rule his maximum tax free cash would have been 120/80ths of earnings, £45,000. His maximum tax-free cash on the formula above would be 15/25 times £45,000 or £27,000.

If 1987 to 1989 – his maximum pension at normal retirement date would have been a strict $1/30^{th}$ for each year of service, but with a maximum of 20 years to count. It would therefore have been 20/30ths of £30,000, £20,000 p.a. His maximum pension based on the formula above would be 15/25 times £20,000, equal to £12,000. He could have taken maximum tax-free cash at retirement, under the normal 80ths limits, of 75/80ths of final salary, £28,125. Under the formula above, his maximum tax-free cash on early retirement would be 15/25 times £28,125 or £16,875. In the same way as for normal retirement, he could only have an increase above this, if the pension being provided, before commutation, was actually to have been more than one sixtieth for each year of service.

Assuming that the scheme was providing him with the maximum accrual rate of 30ths, then as we saw earlier his maximum tax free cash sum at normal retirement date, using the complex formula applicable to 87-89 members would have been given by:

Maximum tax-free cash =

$$\frac{(20,000 - 12,500) \times (45,000 - 28,125)}{(20,000 - 12,500)} + 28,125 = £45,000$$

Applying the formula given in this Appendix for actual service relative to potential service, the actual maximum lump sum allowable is given by 15/25 times £45,000 or £27,000.

If Post-89 – The maximum approvable pension is a strict $1/30^{th}$ for each year of service and therefore it is $15/30^{th}$ of £30,000 or £15,000 per annum. His maximum tax-free cash sum is 2.25 times the pension before any cash sum is taken so is equal to 2.25 times £15,000 or £33,750.

Appendix 3: Retained Benefits from Previous Employments

In Chapter 3, and in Appendices 1 and 2, we have made mention of the concept of retained benefits and referred to benefits out of previous schemes for this purpose.

In more detail, however, retained pension benefits may include:

- Deferred pensions or pensions being paid in respect of previous employment(s), and benefits arising from personal pensions and/or retirement annuities in relation to earlier employments or periods of self-employment. Any protected rights benefits from personal pensions are ignored for this purpose.
- The pension equivalent of any tax-free cash sum received arising out of the membership of a scheme of a previous employer.
- The pension and the pension equivalent of any tax-free cash sum taken from any personal pension scheme or retirement annuity.
- Benefits arising out of any transfer payments that may have been made into the scheme.

Benefits arising out of another concurrent employment do not count so far as the calculation of retained benefits is concerned.

Retained benefits and tax-free cash
For the purposes of the maximum tax-free cash sum, in general terms any retained cash benefits that it may be necessary to take account of are those arising out of any one or more of the above arrangements, and in practice commutation factors will be used to convert such lump sums into pension form.

Retained benefits and taking benefits at different retirement ages

Where the individual's retained benefits are not payable from the same date as the benefits under the occupational scheme, where maximum benefits are being tested taking retained benefits into account, then a notional value for the retained benefit will be taken into account.

This provision will mainly apply where the retained benefit is to be paid at a later date. For example, if an occupational pension scheme member is taking early retirement and the retained benefit is payable from a later date, the retained benefit will be given a discounted value at the earlier date.

Retained benefits and earnings cap

Retained benefits may, however, be completely ignored in relation to pension benefits if in the first year of employment the member's earnings do not exceed a quarter of the earnings cap. Where this test is satisfied, even when the member retires and takes benefits retained, any benefits will be ignored.

This relaxation is not applicable to those who at any time in the last ten years have been controlling (i.e. 20%) directors in respect of the same employment.

Index

A

accumulating net income, staggered vesting 118
actuarial certification, SSAS 154
additional voluntary contributions (AVCs) 9, 51, 53-54
   and tax-free cash 53
allowances, unused 19
annuitant, definition 60
annuities
   conventional. 60–82
   new options 96
   flexible, occupational drawdown 146
   flexible, small self-administered schemes (SSASs) 150
   inflation-linked 75
   unit-linked 76, 95, 102
   unitized with profits 100
   with profits 76, 95, 99
   with profits plus guarantees 100
annuity basis 60
annuity, compulsory purchase 79
annuity, conventional
   and pensions 80
   capital protected 69
   competition 77
   compulsory 78
   deferred 62
   dependant's benefits 67
   escalation rates 71
   expenses 77
   gilt yields 74
   immediate 62
   in advance 61
   in arrears 61
   income, actual level of 77
   joint life 66
   lifetime 70
   mortality 72
   overlap, with or without 69
   payment frequency 61
   payments guaranteed for a minimum period 64
   purchased 78
   purchased life annuities 80
   single life 66
   spouse's benefits 67
   spouse's pension benefit 67
   sub-standard lives 77
   temporary 71
   unit-linked 76
   with or without overlap 69
   with or without proportion 63
   with profits 76
annuity purchase deferral, benefits 154
annuity, purchased life 79
annuity rate 22
   for relatively young 107
   future estimates 121
   risk and pension drawdown 128
appropriate personal pensions (APP) 33, 34
assumed bonus rate, with profits annuities 100
AVCs *see* additional voluntary contributions

B

Barber v. GRE 8
beneficiary, selecting with pension drawdown 129
benefit maximum limits 43
benefits
   added, occupational pension schemes 51
   basic pension, occupational pension 43
   FSAVC 54
   in kind 43
   personal pensions 24
   retirement annuities 32
bonus rate, assumed 100

C

capital protected annuity 69
carry back 19
   allowance 19

carry forward 17, 19
  provision 19
cash sum, tax-free 25
certified tax-free cash, revaluation 26
CIMPS *see* contracted in money purchase schemes
commitments, short-term 108
common-law spouse 88, 108
comparative factors in retirement options 156–164
COMPS *see* contracted out money purchase schemes
compulsory purchase annuity 79
contracted in money purchase schemes (CIMPS) 9
contracted out money purchase schemes (COMPS) 9, 57
contracted out schemes 9
contracting out and state pensions 33
contribution, maximum permissible 17
contributions, maximum in retirement annuities 30
controlling director
  special rules 50
  restrictions 50
conventional annuities 60
  payment frequency 61
conventional with profits annuities 99

D

death and occupational drawdown 148
death benefits
  personal pensions 28
  protected rights 37
  staggered vesting 119
death during drawdown period 128
deferred annuity 63
  definition 63
  payment 62
defined benefit
  occupational pension 8
  pension scheme 3
  personal pension 12
  schemes for occupational pension schemes 55
defined contribution
  occupational pension 9
  pension scheme 3

personal pension 12
  structure 8
dependant, definitions 83
dependants' benefits
  annuity payment 67
  personal pensions 29
director pension plans (DPPs) 9
directors, controlling and special rules 50
drawdown, SSAS 151

E

early retirement in occupational pension schemes 48
earnings cap 18, 26
  occupational pension schemes 45
  retirement annuities 31
employers' contributions 20
employment, pensionable 16
EPPs *see* executive pension plans
escalation rates 71
European Court of Justice 93
executive pension plans (EPPs) 9

F

final remuneration
  benefits in kind 43
  occupational pension schemes 42
final salary pension schemes, definition of spouse 84
Finance Act
  1987 (2) 16
  1989 18, 45
flat rate
  occupational pension 8
  pension 3
  state pension 6
flexibility of income and staggered vesting 117
flexible annuities 146
  age limits 147
  and death of the drawdown member 148
  income withdrawal 147
  occupational drawdown 146, 147
  small self-administered schemes (SSASs) 150
free-standing additional voluntary contribution schemes (FSAVCs) 9, 26, 53, 54

benefits 54
  multiple 54
FSAVCS *see* free-standing additional voluntary contribution schemes

G

GAD *see* Government Actuary's Department
gilt rates, falling 95
gilt yields, annuity payments 74
guaranteed minimum pension *see* GMP
Government Actuary's Department (GAD) 36, 125, 147
  Tables 140
guaranteed minimum pension (GMP) 35, 56
  test 56
guaranteed payment period, annuity 64
guarantees in unit linked annuities 102

H

health, poor or ill 49, 108

I

ill-health and early retirement 49
immediate annuity 62
  definition 62
  annuity payment 62
  e vesting 22
    annuity rate 22
    annuities 17
in advance, annuity payment 61
in arrears, annuity payment 61
Income and Corporation Taxes Act
  1970, Section 226 30
  1988 16
    Chapter III 30
    Section 646 17
income flexibility and staggered vesting 117
income withdrawal and protected rights 36
inflation-linked annuities 75
investment return and staggered vesting 121
investment risk in pension drawdown 143

J

joint life annuity payment 66

L

late retirement, occupational pension schemes 47
legislation for retirement annuities 30
life, single or joint annuity payment 66
lifetime annuity 70
Lisa Grant v. South West Trains 89, 91
living together clause 87

M

maximum benefit limits in occupational pension schemes 43
minimum purchase price in pension drawdown 131
money purchase occupational pension schemes 57
  definition of spouse 84
money purchase structure 8
mortality and annuities 72
mortality drag 129
  pension drawdown 132
  principle 132
  worked example 133
mortality gain in pension drawdown 135
Mrs Margorrian case 8
multiple FSAVCs 54

N

National Insurance contribution 6
  rebates 33
net relevant earnings 17, 18
normal retirement age in occupational pension schemes 42

O

occupational pension drawdown
  and personal pension drawdown 149
  and tax-free cash 149
  eligibility 147
occupational pension schemes 41
  added benefits 51
  and personal pensions 26
  and SERPS 55
  annuities 97
  controlling directors 50
  defined benefit schemes 55
  early retirement 48

179

earnings cap 45
final remuneration 42
increases of benefits 46
late retirement 47
money purchase 57
normal retirement age 42
protected rights 57
service of less than 40 years 45
structure 8
transfers to personal pensions 28
trivial benefits 47
Occupational Pensions Office 16
open market option 27
options, retirement - comparative factors 156–164
overlap, annuity payment with or without 69

P

partners, same-sex 90, 108
pension schemes 1
pension benefit structures 2
Pension Buy Out Bonds 10
pension drawdown
  and desired beneficiary 129
  and interest rates 139
  and investment performance 139
  annuity rate risk 128
  compared to conventional pension annuity 124
  death of a member during period 128
  definition 124
  Government Actuary's Department Tables 140
  investment risk 143
  investment strategy in contract 126
  limits to amount withdrawn 125
  main risks 140
  mortality drag 129, 132
  mortality gain 135
  normal minimum purchase price 131
  occupational 149
  possible restrictions on fund 127
  time limits 131
pension, flat rate 3
pension options 27
pension planning - three pillars 2

pension schemes
  defined benefit 3
  defined contribution 3
  and sexual discrimination 93
pension, state defined
  benefit 6
  contribution 7
pensionable employment 16
pensioners, preserved 86
Pensions Act 1995 8
pensions grid 4, 7, 10, 13
  filling in 5
pensions, occupational 2
  annuities 97
pensions, personal 2
  legislation 16
  permitted contributions 17
  structure 8
Pensions Schemes Office 36
pensions, state 2, 6
pensions vesting, staggered 105–122
permitted contributions to personal pensions 17
personal pensions 2
  and occupational pension scheme 26
  arrangements 15
  benefits available 24
  death benefits 28
  defined benefit 12
  defined contribution 12
  dependants' benefits 29
  drawdown 123–145
  drawdown compared to occupational drawdown 149
  earnings cap 18
  immediate vesting 22
  legislation 16
  open market option 27
  pension options 27
  permitted contributions 17
  structure 12
  transfers from occupational pension schemes 28
  transfers restriction 25
  unused allowances 19
phased retirement 24, 105–122
pillars of pension planning, three 2
preserved pensioners 86

proportion, with or without and annuity payment 63
protected rights 34
   and income withdrawal 36
   benefits 25
   benefits and guarantees 40
   death benefits 37
   occupational pension schemes 57
   restrictions 35
purchased life annuities 79

Q

qualifying spouse 39

R

reducing income but not fully retiring 107
retirement annuities 29
   benefits 32
   earnings cap 31
   eligibility 31
   legislation 30
   maximum permissible contributions 30
   tax-free cash 32
Retirement Benefits Schemes Transfer Values 28
retirement, early 48
retirement, late 47
retirement options
   comparative factors 156–164
   conventional (guaranteed) annuities 157
   occupational pension drawdown 162
   personal pension drawdown 161
   SSAS deferred annuity purchase 163
   staggered vesting 159
   unit-linked annuities 158
   with profit annuities 158
retirement, phased 105–122
retiring before state pension age and staggered vesting 108

S

same-sex partners 90, 108
Section 32 Plan 29
SERPS *see* State Earnings Related Pension Scheme
sexuality discrimination in pension schemes 93
single life annuity payment 66

small self-administered schemes (SSAS) 9, 150
   Actuarial Certification 154
   benefits 151
   deferred annuity purchase 151
   drawdown 151
   drawdown rules 151
   drawing income from fund 152
   investments during drawdown 153
Social Security Act 1986 16
spouse
   at date of death married now 68
   at date of death single now 68
   at retirement 68
   common-law 88
   definition 83
   definition and planning implications 88
   legally married 85, 87
   no qualifying 39
   qualifying 39
   same-sex partners 90
spouse's benefits
   annuity, conventional 67
   annuity payment 67
spouse's pension 38
   buying at age 75 119
   commutation 38
spouse's pension benefit, annuity payment 67
SSAS *see* small self-administered pensions schemes
staggered pensions vesting 105–122
staggered vesting
   accumulating net income 118
   annuity rates based on a relatively young age 107
   availability of tax-free cash 114
   concept 106
   death benefits 119
   investment return 121
   planning in practice 109
   poor health 108
   reasons for 107
   reducing income but not fully retiring 107
   retiring before state pension age 108
   short-term commitments 108
   target income 116

unmarried with partner 108
state defined
   benefit 6
   contribution 7
State Earnings Related Pension Scheme (SERPS) 3, 6, 25, 33
   and occupational pension schemes 55
state pension, flat rate 6
state pensions 2, 6
   and contracting out 33
Statutory Instrument 1990/1142 38
sub-standard lives 77

T

target income in staggered vesting 116
tax-free cash
   and AVCs 53
   and staggered vesting 114
   retirement annuities 32
tax-free cash benefits, basic in occupational pension 44
   sum 25

Taxes Act 16
temporary annuity 71
transfers, restrictions on cash sums 25
Treaty of Rome, Article 119 93
trivial benefits 36
   occupational pension schemes 47

U

unit-linked annuities 76, 95, 102
unitized with profits annuities 100
unused allowances 19
   use of 21
unused relief 17

V

vested segments and choice of annuity basis 118

W

with profits annuities 76, 95, 99
   conventional 99
with profits plus guarantees annuities 100